What Does the Lord Require?

A new anthology of prayers and songs for worship and mission

Compiled by
Francis Brienen

Published in association with
the Council for World Mission

CANTERBURY
PRESS
Norwich

© in this compilation the Council for World Mission 2000

First published in 2000 by The Canterbury Press Norwich
(a publishing imprint of Hymns Ancient & Modern Limited,
a registered charity)
St Mary's Works, St Mary's Plain,
Norwich, Norfolk, NR3 3BH

British Library Cataloguing in Publication Data

A catalogue record for this book is available
from the British Library

ISBN 1-85311-353-0

Typeset by Rowland Phototypesetting,
Bury St Edmunds, Suffolk
Music typeset by Halstan & Co. Ltd,
Amersham, Buckinghamshire
Printed in Great Britain by
Biddles Ltd, Guildford and King's Lynn

Contents

Preface   ix
Introduction   xi

PART 1: PROCLAIMING THE GOOD NEWS

Hymns and Songs

To Christ our hearts now given *by Brian Wren*   1
I'll sing my faith *by Noel Dexter & Susan Heafield*   3
The time has come *by I-to Loh*   5
O what a glorious day! *by Noel Dexter*   7
Enter into God's house *by Noel Dexter*   10
O, worship the Lord *by Noel Dexter*   12

Calls to Worship

Come and receive *by Brian Wren & Susan Heafield*   14
God said, 'Let there be light' *by Brian Wren*   16
We are ambassadors for Christ *by Brian Wren*   16
Follow the King of kings *by Arao Litsure*   17
Christ is the world's true light *by Brian Wren*   17

Invocations

Christ among us *by Brian Wren*   18
We do not proclaim ourselves *by Brian Wren*   19

Prayers

A cloud of witnesses *by Francis Brienen*   20
Prayers for women and men on their journeys
    by Lindsey Sanderson   21
We are the body of Christ *by Brian Wren*   22
Assurance of God's grace *by Brian Wren*   23

God of love, faithful and gracious forever *by Brian Wren*   23
Holy God, hear our cry *by Brian Wren*   24
Call to prayer . . . *by Brian Wren*   25
Let us confess our sin *by Brian Wren*   26
Trinitarian praise and adoration *by Brian Wren*   27
'Here I am, send me' *by Lindsey Sanderson*   28

Litanies

A litany of faith and hope *by Wesley Ariarajah*   29
Celebrating the promises *by Wesley Ariarajah*   31

Symbolic Acts

Gifts for life *by Lindsey Sanderson*   33
Unbinding fear's knots *by Lindsey Sanderson*   33

Stories and Dramas

A better way *by Steven Notis*   35

Blessings

Peace and love *by Noel Dexter*   37
Parent of light, Holy and Good *by Brian Wren*   38
As we go in Christ *by Brian Wren*   38
Let us go in peace *by Brian Wren*   39

PART 2: TRANSFORMING SOCIETY

Hymns and Songs

The Lord has told us what is good *by I-to Loh*   41
This we can do for justice *by Brian Wren & I-to Loh*   43
Building a just society *by James Minchin & I-to Loh*   46
From this time onwards *by I-to Loh & James Minchin*   48
One family *by Noel Dexter*   50
Let justice be our guide *by Brian Wren & Arao Litsure*   52
Eh Vukani (Hey, people of God) *by Arao Litsure*   53
To break the chains
     by Wesley Ariarajah, Brian Wren & I-to Loh   57

Lead us in paths of truth *by Brian Wren & I-to Loh*   58
Living in a world that suffers *by Brian Wren & I-to Loh*   59

Calls to Worship

Listen and look *by Brian Wren*   61
For national occasions *by Brian Wren*   61

Prayers

Gifts *by Francis Brienen*   63
A prayer for Passiontide *by Francis Brienen*   64
Treading down the evils *by Francis Brienen*   65
Confession *by Andrew Williams*   66
A guiding star *by Francis Brienen*   68
An offering prayer *by Brian Wren*   69
Easter affirmation and prayer *by Brian Wren*   69
Easter praise *by Brian Wren*   71

Litanies

Fasting *by Wesley Ariarajah*   72
Break forth together into singing! *by Wesley Ariarajah*   73
The movement of the Spirit
    by Wesley Ariarajah & Lindsey Sanderson   74

Symbolic Acts

Loving God *by Lindsey Sanderson*   79
Come, Holy Spirit *by Lindsey Sanderson*   80
Forgiveness and reconciliation *by Cathy Bott*   81

Complete Liturgies

A service of word and table *by Brian Wren*   83

PART 3: LOVING SERVICE

Hymns and Songs

The washing of the feet *by Jaci C. Maraschin & Brian Wren* 95
Jesus Christ sets free to serve *by I-to Loh*   98

If we love one another *by I-to Loh* 99
Christ's freedom meal *by Brian Wren & I-to Loh* 101
Guaicuru Kyrie *by Simei Monteiro* 103
Loku Famba/Look around you *by Arao Litsure* 105
A Christmas hymn *by Andrew Williams* 106

Calls to Worship

We are the hands of Christ *by Brian Wren* 108

Prayers

A litany of intercession *by Brian Wren* 109
Christ, you meet us *by Brian Wren & I-to Loh* 111
I will follow you wherever you go *by Francis Brienen* 112
The word made flesh *by Francis Brienen* 113
Prayer of intercession *by Andrew Williams* 114
Closing prayer *by Lindsey Sanderson* 117

Symbolic Acts

The circle of love *by Brian Wren* 118
What is love? *by Lindsey Sanderson* 124

Stories and Dramas

The giving tree *by Shel Silverstein* 125
Who is my neighbour? *by Lindsey Sanderson* 126
Stories from Penrhys *by Lindsey Sanderson* 129
Bearing one another's burden *by Cathy Bott* 131

Complete Liturgies

In Jesus' Footsteps *by Simei Monteiro* 132

PART 4: NURTURING AND TEACHING

Hymns and Songs

We meet as friends at table *by Brian Wren & Hal Hopson* 137
Many yet one are the gifts of God's people
   by Lindsey Sanderson & Susan Heafield 139

Remember *by Noel Dexter*   142
The church is like a table *by Fred Kaan & I-to Loh*   145
Tua Palavra é lâmpada *by Simei Monteiro*   147
You are my body *by Brian Wren & John Horman*   149
Here's a new robe *by Brian Wren & Susan Heafield*   152
Holy God, as you love us *by Brian Wren & Susan Heafield*   155
Swamin wahanse *by I-to Loh*   158

Calls to Worship

Fed by community . . . *by Lindsey Sanderson*   159
Living in unity . . . *by Lindsey Sanderson*   159
People of the Covenant, draw near *by Brian Wren*   160

Prayers

An invitation to the banquet *by Francis Brienen*   161
Living One, we belong to you *by Brian Wren*   162
May the Lover of Creation *by Brian Wren*   162
Christ, our Teacher *by Brian Wren*   163
An opening prayer *by Brian Wren*   163
A prayer of confession *by CWM*   163
The road to Emmaus *by Francis Brienen*   165

Stories and Dramas

The story of the hand *by Lindsey Sanderson*   167
The rainbow *by Lindsey Sanderson & EEA*   168

Complete Liturgies

We all belong to Christ's Body *by I-to Loh*   171
A communion meditation
    by Simei Monteiro & Lindsey Sanderson   175

PART 5: CARING FOR CREATION

Hymns and Songs

The God of us all *by Ron O'Grady & I-to Loh*   177
Thank you, God, for water, soil and air *by Brian Wren*   179

Send out your Spirit *by Brian Wren & Simei Monteiro*   181
God's glory (praise) *by Brian Wren & Susan Heafield*   183
Earth is abused (repentance) *by Brian Wren & Susan Heafield*   185
Can we believe . . .? (thanksgiving)
   by Brian Wren & Susan Heafield   187
We praise you, O God *by Noel Dexter*   189
O, forgive us, dear Lord *by Noel Dexter*   189
We praise you, we thank you *by Noel Dexter*   189
Loving God, forgive *by Andrew Williams*   190

Calls to Worship

The earth belongs to God *by Brian Wren*   191
Our Creator calls us *by Brian Wren*   192
In the beginning God said . . . *by Cathy Bott*   192

Prayers

A prayer of confession *by Cathy Bott*   193
A prayer of commitment *by Cathy Bott*   193
Bright and beautiful God *by Francis Brienen*   194

Litanies

A litany on creation *by Wesley Ariarajah*   196

Symbolic Acts

Modelling *by Lindsey Sanderson*   199

Stories and Dramas

Miss World visits the doctor *by Lindsey Sanderson*   200
Greyfriars Bobby *by Lindsey Sanderson*   203

Acknowledgements   204

Preface

Nine hymn writers, musicians and liturgists from around the world came together to create this new resource for worship. For five inspiring and music filled days they wrote songs and prayers, composed tunes to new and existing hymns and dreamed up dramas and symbolic acts. This book is theirs. They have created it and my sincere thanks go to all of them.

Wesley Ariarajah from Sri Lanka is Professor of Ecumenical Theology at Drew University in New Jersey, USA. For many years he worked for the World Council of Churches as Director of the Interfaith Dialogue Programme and was involved in organising worship for WCC Assemblies and other meetings.

Cathy Bott from South Africa is the convenor of the mission council of the United Congregational Church of Southern Africa with special responsibility for worship and liturgy.

Noel Dexter from Jamaica is Director of Music at the University of the West Indies in Kingston. He has composed many songs and hymns, and directs the internationally known University Singers.

Arao Litsure from Mozambique is a professional musician and a minister. He serves the United Congregational Church of Southern Africa as Synod Secretary for Mozambique. He uses his musical talent as a means to reach out to young people.

I-to Loh from Taiwan has collected and created many worship resources that are contextual to Asia. Trained as an ethnomusicologist, he is currently the principal of the Tainan Theological College.

Simei Monteiro from Brazil teaches liturgy in the Methodist University of Sao Paulo where she also co-ordinates the Pastoral Institute.

Simei's work has been published in a number of worship books, song collections and hymnals in Brazil and elsewhere.

Lindsey Sanderson is a minister of the United Reformed Church in the UK. She serves as mission enabler in the Scotland Synod and equips local churches for involvement in mission.

Brian Wren and **Susan Heafield** from the USA are partners in marriage and ministry. Brian is a minister of the United Reformed Church in the UK and an internationally published hymn writer. He was recently appointed as Professor of Worship at Columbia Theological Seminary in Decatur, Georgia, USA.

Susan is a minister in the United Methodist Church. Prior to ordination she taught music, piano, voice and guitar. She has served congregations in Pennsylvania, New York and Maine, and now has an appointment in the North Georgia Conference.

I am also more than grateful to Zoe Nobes and Madeline Schofield. They pursued copyright permissions, corresponded with authors, typed and ordered materials. Without their persistence and commitment this book would not have come about.

Francis Brienen

Francis Brienen is Associate Secretary for Training and Education for the Council for World Mission, a responsibility which involves her in young peoples' work and developing women's leadership in many Third World countries.

Introduction

In Tokelau in the Pacific, translators employed by the church have just completed a translation of Mark's Gospel and are continuing to work on the other gospels, and Acts and Romans. Having large parts of the New Testament in the local language will greatly enhance the witness of the church.

In North and South Korea the churches are leading the way in developing partnerships across the divided peninsula. Church leaders from the North and the South visit one another and discuss reunification and peace policies. Efforts are being made to reunite families who were divided after the truce in 1953.

In India a Christian doctor has set up a private practice for women involved in the sex trade in a poor predominantly Muslim community. Together with others she has established a project to offer the women health, education and economic empowerment.

In Jamaica and the Cayman Islands the United Church is encouraging youth groups to be self-running. In that way the young people can explore issues of faith and life in ways they want. They learn from each other, nurture one another in faith and build up a strong sense of fellowship.

In Zambia the United Church has become involved in bee-keeping. The bee-keeping project buys honey from farmers and uses it to make beeswax products which are sold in shops or to churches. Keeping bees is an environmentally friendly form of farming and a good way of supporting the church in mission.

These experiences from around the world show that more and more churches are rediscovering their call to mission. They no longer view mission as the responsibility of 'experts' sent abroad by missionary societies. Rather, they see it as their own responsibility. They are called to be the face of Christ in their own local communities. And being the face of Christ can take many forms. It involves proclaiming the Good News, as in Tokelau. It means trying to overcome the injustices of the past, as in Korea, or nurturing young people in the faith, as in Jamaica. Whenever the church is reaching out in the power of the Spirit to witness, serve, nurture, change society or care for creation it is engaged in mission.

'*What Does the Lord Require?*' is for people and churches in mission. It is for churches who would like to hold their worship and their mission engagement together. I have been to many churches around the world who were very active in their communities or very involved in issues of global justice. However, in the Sunday service you would have been hard-pressed to notice that this was the case. Yet, worship is the joyful celebration of life in the world, our response to what God has done and is doing in our lives, our communities and our world. In worship we gather together to be shaped as communities that seek to live out the gospel. In worship we place ourselves within a vision of a different world and make ourselves part of the process that will bring that new reality about. As such worship is the heartbeat of mission. It is not an interruption in the church's participation in mission. Rather it is an essential part of being on the way. It is nourishment for churches on their mission journey.

'*What Does the Lord Require?*' has been created by an international group of people who gathered for a workshop in which they wrote new songs, composed tunes to new and existing hymns, submitted materials not published before (and sometimes written by other authors), and revised older materials. What they aimed to create was a worship resource for people who are on a mission journey and who seek to be nourished on the way; people who are inspired by the words of the prophet Micah, 'He has told you, O mortal, what is good; and what does the Lord require of you but to do justice, and to love kindness, and to walk humbly with your God?' (Micah 6:8).

'*What does the Lord Require?*' has been organised in five sections. Each section focuses on one of the five marks of mission that are now commonly used in many churches: proclaiming the Good News, transforming society, loving service, nurturing and teaching, and caring for creation. The items included follow a set order. Each section starts with hymns and songs, followed by calls to worship, prayers, litanies, symbolic acts, stories and dramas, blessings and/or complete liturgies. Although much of the material can be used for private reflection, most of it is best used in public worship or in small groups. Many items are suitable for use with children or young people, especially the songs, symbolic acts and the stories and dramas. The material included is ecumenical in nature, which is visible in the variety of languages, and the verbal, musical and denominational styles used. This book also encourages active participation of the congregation in worship and for that reason a large number of responsive prayers and items that require a number of leaders (and at times the whole congregation) has been included. The symbolic actions, stories and dramas will enable you to create worship that appeals to all ages and involves not only sight and hearing but other senses as well.

Using the materials in the book will require some creativity. As the materials have been written from the authors' perspectives, they may require some adaptation to your own context. Where this is the case, this has been indicated. Singing the new songs will require some preparation (and a bit of boldness!) on the part of the worship or music leader. The songs included come from many countries but in all cases an English translation has been provided. In some cases a translation that is not for singing has been given and you are encouraged to sing the songs in their original language. The pronunciation is phonetic. Where songs are written in a musical style not familiar to you, we encourage you to try them anyway, and to persist. The result will be worth it. Dramas, litanies and some other items involve several participants. When using these, a rehearsal beforehand is advised. Wherever items include Biblical references, the New Revised Standard Version has been used, unless otherwise stated.

'What does the Lord Require?' is not a book to be read from beginning to end. Rather, it is a book to dip into as you prepare for worship or in your own quiet time. How it is used is ultimately up to you and your context. One thing, however, should be borne in mind. If the words and music offered here are used only as an alternative to mission engagement, no matter how appropriate they are, then they are misused. Micah's question was preceded by another one and serves as a reminder. 'With what', did he ask himself, 'shall I come before the Lord?' The answer was unequivocal: not with burnt offerings but with acts of justice and kindness.

Prayer

We are called and gathered to celebrate God's saving grace
and live joyfully as signs of the Kingdom.
We are called and gathered as people created,
redeemed and empowered to share the love of Christ.
We are called and gathered in the name of the Spirit
to give witness to the transforming power of God in the world.
We are called and gathered to reflect, pray
and respond obediently to what the Lord requires.
May our hearts and minds, attitudes and will be open to God.
Amen.

Francis Brienen

Part 1

Proclaiming the Good News

Hymns and Songs

To Christ our hearts now given

Words: Brian Wren
Music: Johann Steurlein, 1575

WIE LIEBLICH IST DER MAIEN
7.6.7.6.D. *Iambic*

1. To Christ our hearts now given, we join in joyful praise, and pray, in all our living, to grow in loving ways. The

free - ing grace that_ found us, God's heal - ing,

win - ning_ call, in free - dom now_ has_

bound us to love and give our all.

2. From many tribes and places,
   with thankful songs we come
   to blend our gifts and graces,
   and pray and work as one.
   We vow, whate'er betide us,
   in love and truth to stay,
   for Christ moves on beside us,
   and guides us on our way.

3. Wherever we may venture
   to witness, heal and care,
   the Spirit of our Saviour
   has long been lodging there.
   Then let us give with gladness,
   not claiming to deserve
   the wisdom, strength and kindness
   of those we kneel to serve.

4. The freeing grace that found us,
   the love that makes us one,
   is ranging far beyond us,
   and bids us travel on
   to share God's great salvation,
   defend our neighbour's worth,
   dismantle domination,
   and heal our aching earth.

2

I'll sing my faith

Words: Noel Dexter

Music: Susan Heafield

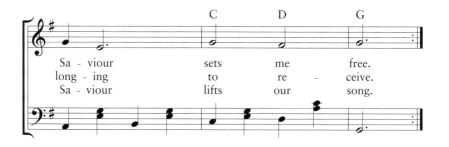

Sa - viour sets me free.
long - ing to re - ceive.
Sa - viour lifts our song.

The time has come

(Mark 1:15)

I-to Loh

The time has come, the realm of God is near. Repent and believe in the good news. Proclaim the gospel through teach-ing, heal - ing,

feed - ing,   and   car -   -   ing.

O what a glorious day!

Noel Dexter

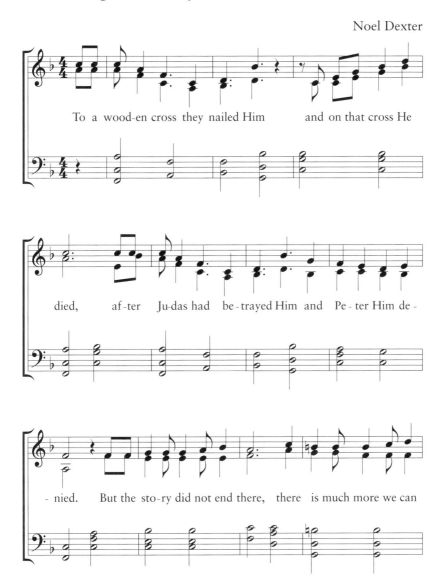

To a wood-en cross they nailed Him and on that cross He died, af-ter Ju-das had be-trayed Him and Pe-ter Him de- nied. But the sto-ry did not end there, there is much more we can

tell. For He burst the chains of death and hell and all is well.

Quicker

There was a re - surr - ec - tion morn - ing,_____

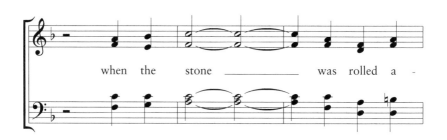

when the stone _____ was rolled a -

- way, _____ When Je - sus my

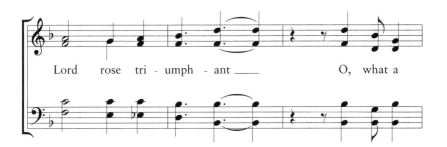

Lord rose tri - umph - ant ____ O, what a

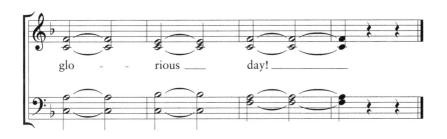

glo - - rious ____ day! ____

So when burdens are too heavy,
When no more you can bear,
When your trials have you nailed down
And no one seems to care,
You can write your own story too,
So those who read it can tell
How His Power working in your soul
Made all things well.

Enter into God's house

Noel Dexter

En - ter in - to God's house   with   songs   of   praise ____ En - ter in - to God's house   with   songs   of   praise.   For   He is   the Lord our   Ma - ker.   He is   the Lord our   Ma - ker.   He is   the Lord our

Ma - ker, En - ter his house with praise._____

O, worship the Lord

Music: Noel Dexter

Words: J.S.B. Monsell
1811–75 (altered)

O, wor - ship the Lord in the beau - ty of ho - li-ness. Bow down be - fore Him, His glo - ry pro - claim: With gold of o - be - dience and in - cense of low - li-ness,

kneel and a - dore Him, the Lord is His name.

Calls to worship

Come and Receive (may be said or sung)

Leader: Come and receive
All: **Come and receive**
Leader: hope and good news!
All: **hope and good news!**
Leader: Come and believe
All: **Come and believe**
Leader: Christ is alive.
All: **Christ is alive.**
Leader: Then we will go
All: **Then we will go**
Leader: giving good news.
All: **giving good news.**
Leader: Thanks be to God!
All: **Thanks be to God!**

Words: Brian Wren   Music: Susan Heafield

15

God said, 'Let there be light!'

Based on 2 Corinthians 4:6.

Leader: God said, 'Let there be light,'
             and time and space exploded and began.
Response: Thanks be to God!
Leader: God said, 'Let there be light,'
             and Jesus was shining in our hearts.
Response: Thanks be to God!

Brian Wren

We are ambassadors for Christ

Based on 2 Corinthians 5:20.

Leader: We are ambassadors for Christ.
Response: Fill our hearts with your love.
Leader: We are ambassadors for Christ.
Response: Fill our hearts with your love.
Leader: We are ambassadors for Christ.
Response: Send us out with a song!

Brian Wren

Follow the King of kings

Arao Litsure

Lo - ku u-la-nze - la Ho - si ya ti Ho — si

U - ta ku-ma a —— wu to - mi

If you follow the King of kings you will have life.

Christis the world's true light

'Christ is the world's true light,
its captain of salvation,
the daystar clear and bright,
desire of every nation.' –
We assemble in the name of Christ our Saviour,
centre of the church,
cornerstone of salvation,
hinge of human hope,
who chooses to be centred,
not in the circles of privilege and power,
but at the margin,
with the downtrodden, the rejected, and the despised.
We shall tell the story of God's mighty work in Christ
and offer our worship and praise.
Let us worship God.

Brian Wren

Invocations

Christ among us

Spoken over the quietly played tune of 'Kum Bayah'.

Spirit of Jesus, Spirit of God, Christ among us,
when we say, 'Come,' you already sit beside us.
When we say, 'Lead us,' you already go before us.
When we say, 'Guide us,' you already nudge us and call us.
Yet we say, 'Come and lead us, come and guide us,'
that we may know and praise
your presence and promise.

Light of the World, radiant with love,
Living water, overflowing with justice,
      Christ, our Rescuer, come . . .
First-Born of Creation,
Gardener of New Life,
      Christ, our Healer, come . . .
Seeker of lost coins, and lost sheep,
Healer of children, Friend of women,
      Christ, our Companion, come . . .
Wisdom and Word of God,
Rabbi incomparable,
      Christ, our Teacher, come.
Lover of outcasts,
Disconcerting Comforter,
Footwasher and Friend,
      Christ, our Leader, come.
Crucified and Risen,
Endlessly Alive,
Taming Emptiness and Evil,
      Christ, our Life-Giver, come.

Brian Wren

We do not proclaim ourselves

From 1 Corinthians 4–5.

Leader: We do not proclaim ourselves.
We proclaim Jesus Christ as Lord
and ourselves as your slaves
for Jesus' sake.

East: When anyone is in Christ, there is a new creation.
Everything old has passed away.
Everything has become new.

West: But we have this treasure in earthen jars,
to show that the extraordinary power
comes from God, and does not come from us.

East: We are ambassadors of Christ,
entrusted with the message of reconciliation.

West: Therefore, since it is by God's mercy
that we are engaged in this ministry,
we will not lose heart.

All: **Thanks be to God!**

Brian Wren

Prayers

A cloud of witnesses

Before you, O God,
we remember the ones who went before us,
who followed you with tenacity and joy.
Full of courage and trust,
they went to new places,
to stand and suffer with you.

**Like a cloud of many witnesses
they stand around us.**

Before you, O God,
we remember the saints of today,
who do not live by the rigid letter of the law
but by the wild demands of faith,
always prepared to give more,
always prepared to be turned inside out,
knowing that new ways can only be found
through risk and pain.

**Like a cloud of many witnesses
they stand around us.**

Eternal God,
we thank you for the witnesses of all times and all places.
May the stories of their lives show us the richness of your grace.
May they inspire us to look deep within our souls.
May they encourage us to take the risk of faith
and to serve you in new ways.

Francis Brienen

Prayers for women and men on their journeys

Creating and sustaining God,
as we were formed in our mothers' wombs,
and as we have travelled each step of life's path,
You have journeyed with us.
As we have struggled to feel your presence,
and as we have seen you in friend and stranger,
You have journeyed with us.
As we have rejoiced in your creating love,
and felt the pain of your world's suffering,
You have journeyed with us.
As we live in this moment and look to the future,
we are sure in our conviction that you will journey with us.

We pause to remember with thankfulness
those who have journeyed before us,
whose stories we have heard and draw strength from:
Sarah, who left her world
and travelled into the unknown with Abraham,
Miriam, who sang and danced for the Lord,
Deborah, whose wisdom guided the ancient Hebrew people,
Ruth, who challenged an inward-looking society,
Elizabeth, who offered support to Mary during her pregnancy,
Martha, who professed her faith, in the midst of her grief,
Mary, the mother of John Mark,
who offered her home as a place of prayer.

As we journey on, women and men together,
may we listen with compassion
to the stories that each of us has to tell.
May we rejoice in the diversity of gifts,
reflections of your image,
which have been given to each of us.
And may we be led forward as partners in mission,
offering worship and witness to God,
who is both father and mother of us all.

We offer our prayers in the name of Jesus,
God's son and our brother.
Amen.

Lindsey Sanderson

We are the body of Christ

We are the body of Christ,
needing forgiveness and transformation.
If we say we are without sin, we deceive ourselves,
and the truth is not in us.
If we confess our sins, God is just,
and may be trusted to forgive our sins,
and cleanse us from every kind of wrong.

(Silence for preparation.)

God calls us in love, and calls us to account,
judging with love, and loving in judgement.
As we say what we have often said before,
let light shine, and doors be opened:

**Holy and Loving God,
we have gone wrong, and gone astray,
by choice and by conditioning,
in ignorance, and in awareness,
by ourselves, and with others.
We take responsibility, and ask forgiveness.
By your Spirit, turn us from evil to good.
Give us a clean heart, and a new start,
as we make amends, forgive others,
and walk in truth and love,
through Jesus Christ,
our Partner, Friend and Saviour. Amen.**

In repentance and faith
receive the promise:
'Jesus Christ came into the world to save sinners.'
God loves and values us, forgives what is past,
and calls us to new discipleship.
Thanks be to God!

Brian Wren

Assurance of God's grace

God's love is costly, generous, and trustworthy,
deeper than our expectations, higher than our hopes.
Accept in your heart the promise of new life,
and proclaim with your lips
the inexhaustible goodness of God:

Holy, Holy, Holy,
Love's empowering might,
heaven and earth are full of your glory.
We give you glory, God most high!

Brian Wren

God of love, faithful and gracious forever

God of Love, faithful and gracious forever,
we thank you and praise you.
You love us more than we love ourselves.
You believe in us more than we believe in ourselves.
You call us onward with Christ,
to be more than we ever thought possible.
Take our gifts. Receive our thanks.
Accept our praise.
Through Jesus Christ.
Amen.

Brian Wren

Holy God, hear our cry

One: Holy God, hear our cry.

All: If we are in bondage
to systems and dominant cultures,
to people who hurt us,
to our needs and addictions,
and to ingrained patterns of wrong,
hear us and help us.

One: Holy God, hear our cry.

All: If we are separated from each other,
separated from our true selves,
caught in emptiness and loss,
hear us and help us.

One: Holy God, hear our cry.

All: If we have hidden from you,
or turned against you,
wasting our opportunities,
breaking our promises,
hurting others, and ourselves,
hear us and help us.

One: Hear the good news:
in Christ God brings us
forgiveness and healing for all,
a way out of exile, that brings everyone home,
a way out of bondage, that will never enslave others.
Accept in your heart, and proclaim on your lips,
the new covenant in Jesus Christ.

All: Alleluia! God is Love!
Alleluia! Christ is Risen!
Alleluia! The Spirit is with us!
God be praised!
Amen.

Brian Wren

Call to prayer

Dear friends,
we are created in the image and likeness of God:
women and men, girls and boys,
the oldest and the youngest.
Here and now, through Jesus Christ,
God loves us, and reaches out to us
with unbounded love and amazing grace.
So let us pray in honesty and trust,
gladly accountable,
seeking forgiveness,
believing that today, for us,
there can be new beginnings,
new hope, and new life.

Prayer of confession

God of all nations,
we praise you that in Jesus Christ
the barriers between people are torn down,
as your Spirit plants the seeds of peace and hope.
We grieve with you at the hatreds and hurts of our world.
We confess our slowness and reluctance
to welcome people of other customs, religions and languages.
Free us from fear of the foreigner
and shyness with strangers,
that we may move toward the day
when all are truly one.

Words of assurance

Here is good news.
Christ came from one people, for all people.
Christ comes to all of us, whoever we are,
and whatever we have done,
and says, 'Peace be with you.
I am with you. Follow me!'
Believe, and be thankful.

Brian Wren

Let us confess our sin

Let us confess our sin against God and our neighbours.
Living and loving God,
we confess that we have gone against you
in thought, word and deed,
by what we have done, or failed to do.
We have not loved you with our whole heart,
we have not loved our neighbours as ourselves.
And we admit with sadness
our captivity to social unfairness,
and to forces beyond our control.
By your love in Jesus Christ,
forgive us, help us, and strengthen us,
that we may delight in your will, and walk in your way,
to the glory of your name. Amen.

(Silence.)

Be assured that God knows you, loves you,
forgives you, and receives you.
May the Holy Spirit rest upon you,
and keep you in eternal life. Amen.

Brian Wren

Trinitarian praise and adoration

Creator God, Lover of Creation,
giver of food and drink, clothing and warmth,
love and hope, life in all its goodness:
>**We praise and adore you.**

Jesus our Lord, Wisdom and Word,
lover of outcasts, friend of the poor,
one of us, yet one with God,
crucified and risen, life in the midst of death:
>**We praise and adore you.**

Holy Spirit, storm and breath,
building bridges, breaking chains,
opening doors, waking the oppressed,
unseen and unexpected,
untameable energy of life:
>**We praise and adore you.**

Holy Trinity, source of all sharing,
in whom we love, and meet, and know our neighbour,
Oneness-by-Communion, unbounded dance of love,
life in all its fullness, making all things new:
>**With heart and mind and voice**
>**We praise and adore you.**

Brian Wren

'Here I am, send me'

Read Isaiah 6:1–8

Living God, you call out our names,
'Who will go for us?'

Here I am, send me.

We, young and old, women and men,
with different gifts and skills,
people of every place and nation,
speaking many languages,
sharing many life stories.

'Who will go for us?'

Here I am, send me.

Living God, you send us out.
Out amongst our families and friends,
out into our communities, towns and cities,
out to live, mix and mingle with others.
You send us out with love and joy and hope,
to pour cups of tea and play with children,
to listen to worried parents and deliver the church newsletter,
to sign justice petitions and recycle glass bottles.

You send us out to share in your mission,
wherever and whoever we are.

Living God, you call out our names,
'Who will go for us?'

Here I am. Send me.

Lindsey Sanderson

Litanies

A litany of faith and hope

Leader: Therefore, since we are justified by faith, we have peace
with God through our Lord Jesus Christ . . . and we
boast in the hope of sharing the glory of God. And not
only that, but we also boast in our suffering, knowing
that suffering produces endurance, and endurance
produces character, and character produces hope, and
hope does not disappoint us, because God's love has
been poured into our hearts through the Holy Spirit
that has been given to us.

(Romans 5:1–5)

Witness I: *(A contemporary story of faith and hope in the midst
of suffering.)*

Leader: For in hope we were saved. Now hope that is seen is
not hope. For who hopes for what is seen? But if we
hope for what we do not see, we wait for it with
patience . . . What then are we to say about these
things? If God is for us, who is against us? . . . No, in
all these things we are more than conquerors through
him who loved us.

(Romans 8:24–39)

Witness II: *(A story of hope in the midst of fear and death.)*

Leader: Now faith is the assurance of things hoped for, the
conviction of things not seen . . . By faith Abraham
obeyed when he was called to set out for a place that
he was to receive as an inheritance; and he set out, not
knowing where he was going.
      By faith Moses left Egypt, unafraid of the king's

29

anger; for he persevered as though he saw him who is invisible . . . And what more should I say? For time would fail me to tell of Gideon, Barak, Samson, Jephthah, of David and Samuel and the prophets – who through faith conquered kingdoms, administered justice, obtained promises . . .

Others were tortured, refusing to accept release, in order to obtain a better resurrection. Others suffered mocking and flogging, and even chains and imprisonment . . .

(Hebrews 11)

Witness III: *(The congregation is asked to write on sheets of paper, hung on the wall, their roll-call of faith – people whose life has inspired them, who have given their life for their convictions and who have suffered in the course of defending the rights of people.)*

Leader: Therefore, since we are surrounded by so great a cloud of witnesses, let us also lay aside every weight and the sin that clings so closely, and let us run with perseverance the race that is set before us, looking to Jesus, the pioneer and perfector of our faith . . .

(Hebrews 12:1–2)

(Silence.)

Leader: Blessed be the God and Father of our Lord Jesus Christ! By his great mercy he has given us a new birth into a living hope through the resurrection of Jesus Christ from the dead, and into an inheritance that is imperishable, undefiled and unfading . . . Come to him, a living stone, though rejected by mortals yet chosen and precious in God's sight, and like living stones, let yourselves be built into a spiritual house, to be a holy priesthood to offer spiritual sacrifices acceptable to God through Jesus Christ.

(1 Peter 1:3–4; 2:4–5)

| People: | But you are a chosen race, a royal priesthood, a holy nation, God's own people, in order that we may proclaim the mighty acts of him who called you out of darkness into his marvellous light. Once you were not a people, but now we are God's people; once we had not received mercy, but now we have received mercy. |

(1 Peter 2:9–10)

| Leader: | Thanks be to God. |

| **All:** | **Amen.** |

Wesley Ariarajah

Celebrating the promises

(L = Leader. P = People.)

L: In the midst of ignorance, prejudice and suspicion
    that have fractured life in community,

P: we celebrate the promise of healing and unity.

L: In the midst of injustice, oppression and tyranny
    that enslave people's lives,

P: we celebrate the promise of justice and freedom.

L: In the midst of bitterness, hatred and war
    that threaten the human family,

P: we celebrate the promise of reconciliation and peace.

L: In the midst of hunger, disease and suffering
    that crush the spirit of people,

P: we celebrate the promise of love and hope.

L: In the midst of sin and greed, decay and death
that rob life of its meaning,

P: we celebrate the promise of renewal and life.

All: In the midst of doubt and despair on every side,
we celebrate the promise of the Living Christ.

Wesley Ariarajah

Symbolic Acts

Gifts for life

Biblical basis: 'You must shine among them like stars lighting up the sky, as you offer them the message of life' (Philippians 2:15–16, Good News Bible).

Each person is given a paper star which has a thread through it. At the appropriate point in the service people are invited to write down or draw their particular gift which offers the word of life to others. This could range from very specific gifts to more general gifts of friendship, being a good neighbour, being faithful to God's word. Children and young people could be involved.

The stars should then be gathered together and suspended from a higher string or series of strings so that it is possible to see a mass of stars as you might do on a clear evening.

Lindsey Sanderson

Unbinding fear's knots

Introduction

The worship leader explains that at times we are all frightened of something or someone. He or she may give examples and invite others to add examples from their experience. Ensure that the children are involved in giving examples too.

Facing Our Fears

Long pieces of cloth are then passed round the congregation. All are invited to think of a fear and in recognition of that fear tie a loose knot in the piece of cloth when it comes to them. A link can be made with the feeling of 'knots' in our stomachs when we are frightened. The cloths are then gathered together.

Reading

God's promise in Isaiah 43:1b is read:

'Do not fear, for I have redeemed you;
I have called you by name, you are mine'.

A short meditation can be given on the special nature of God's promises (i.e. they are not broken) and on the fact that God knows each of us by name.

Handing Our Fears To God

The pieces of cloth are then redistributed and people are invited to untie one knot from the cloth as it comes to them, and in so doing hand their fears to God.

During the untying the words of Isaiah 43:1b can be used as a sung chant (see *Mission Praise*, no. 41).

Lindsey Sanderson

Stories and Dramas

A better way

This is a true story. For obvious reasons, names and places are withheld.

Walking across the parking lot early on Sunday morning, the pastor wondered what he would find. Twice during the past week, the church had been broken into and vandalized – an unheard-of event for a small town in southern Maine, USA.

On the Wednesday before last, the choir's bookshelf had been pushed over, and hymnals and sheet music strewn across the floor. Arriving early last Sunday morning, the pastor had found a congealed mess of sugar, ketchup, vinegar, milk, coffee and juice all over the kitchen floor. Was it an anti-church hate crime? Had one of the members 'gone off the deep end'? Anger, hurt and suspicion shrouded the church community.

Opening the door, the pastor's worst fears were realized. Potted plants had been slashed to stubs. The kitchen walls, floor, and ceiling were covered with food. In the library, sofa and wing chairs had been slashed. Someone had defecated in the storage room. In the sanctuary, the cross had been thrown down from the altar. Someone had urinated on the organ. Furniture and floors were covered with white powder: every fire extinguisher in the building had been discharged.

The police arrived, collected evidence, and said that the town's middle school had also been vandalized. 'I hate to admit it,' said the pastor, 'but I immediately felt relief. At least it wasn't a hate-crime, nor a disturbed church member.' Even so, pastor and congregation were shocked and hurt. Their sacred space had been violated, for no apparent reason.

Volunteers cleaned up, and they held Sunday worship. It was important to worship, especially now. Later that week, they heard that three boys, two twelve and one thirteen, had confessed to the crimes. Two were brothers.

In the following weeks, the pastor began to feel angry at the boys

35

and their parents. No one apologized: later, he learned that legal counsel had advised against contact. The boys pleaded 'not guilty' to crimes they had previously confessed. 'Not for the first time,' the pastor said, 'we experienced the legal system as counter to the deeper needs of victim and offender. As victims it felt like it was all a game.'

Frustration prompted him to seek a better way. Making enquiries, he found that two of the boys – the brothers – had been advised to try victim/offender mediation (the third boy had psychological problems, so probably wouldn't benefit). To the congregation, the prospect of meeting the boys came as a relief. Finally they might be able to understand and move on – perhaps even help.

Who would represent the church? What would the agenda be? The congregation found it hard to reach agreement. Finally, they decided to let different voices and viewpoints speak. Then they waited, with anxiety and hope.

On the day, the boys, parents and members of the congregation met in the presence of a mediator. Church members said how hurt they were, and why. The boys tried to explain why they had done what they did. They felt, and showed, shame at their behaviour. A programme of work service was agreed, which the boys would carry out.

'Best of all,' said the pastor, 'they became people to us. No longer were they faceless little demons who trashed our church, but two boys who had admitted their mistake and were working to make amends. It took a great deal of courage for them and their parents and I will always respect them for it.'

A few weeks after mediation the boys and their parents joined the congregation on Sunday morning. When they came forward for communion, many were moved to tears.

The family continues in relationship with the church. They are in worship most Sundays. The boys have joined the church's youth programme.

Mediation led to forgiveness and healing. Church members no longer describe the pair as 'the boys who trashed our church'. Nowadays, they call them by name.

Revd Steven M. Notis

Blessings

Peace and love

Jamaican traditional.

Noel Dexter

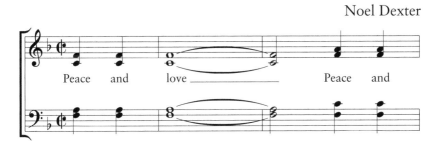

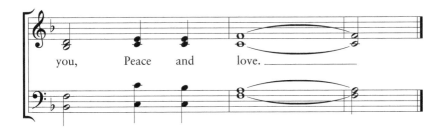

Parent of Light, Holy and Good

Parent of Light, Holy and Good,
we come to you with unclean lips,
and find ourselves loved, valued and made whole.
> **We praise and adore you, and go in your name.**

Living Partner, Christ our Hope,
in your life and death we meet new life
and have good news for the whole world.
> **We praise and adore you, and go in your name.**

Spirit of Jesus, Spirit of God,
by your love we become one body,
called out of hiding into wholeness.
> **We praise and adore you, and go in your name.**

Mysterious God, in whom we live and move,
help us to leave our tangled nets
and go where you lead us,
through Christ, in the power of the Spirit. Amen.

Brian Wren

As we go in Christ

One: As we go in Christ,
        let us handle Christ's Name with love,
All: **Not as a hammer for hammering**
        but as bread for sharing.

One: Let us speak Christ's Name in praise,
All: **Not as a battle-cry**
        but as a love-song.

One: Let us carry Christ's Name with care,
All: **Not as a sword**
        but as a cross.

One: May the Gifted One relieve you,
        May the Given One retrieve you,
        May the Giving One receive you,
        Three in One, joy in life unending.

All: **Amen.**

Brian Wren

Let us go in peace

(This is part of the 'Service of Word and Table', p. 83.)

Let us go in peace,
To act justly, love mercy,
And walk humbly with God.
May the Giver of Law,
The Word of Grace,
And the Breath of Life, One God,
Help us love justice, trust love,
And live faithfully,
Through Jesus Christ, our Saviour.

Brian Wren

Part 2

Transforming Society

Hymns and Songs

The Lord has told us what is good

Chú bat chí-sī sím-mĭh sī hó

Words: Micah 6:8
Music: I-to Loh

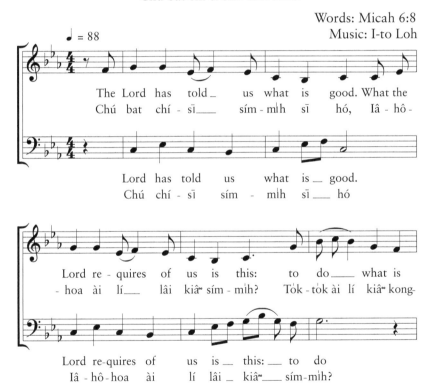

♩ = 88

The Lord has told us what is good. What the
Chú bat chí - sī sím - mĭh sī hó, Iâ - hô -

Lord has told us what is good.
Chú chí - sī sím - mĭh sī hó

Lord re - quires of us is this: to do what is
- hoa ài lí lâi kiâⁿ sím - mĭh? Tŏk - tŏk ài lí kiâⁿ kong-

Lord re - quires of us is this: to do
Iâ - hô - hoa ài lí lâi kiâⁿ sím - mĭh?

just, to show constant love and to
gī, tok-tok ài lí sim chûn lîn - bín, ài khiam-

what is just, to show con - stant love and to
ài lí kiâⁿ kong-gī, ài lí chûn lîn - bín,

rit.

live in hum - ble fe - low - ship with our God.
- pi kap lí ê Chú Sióng - tè saⁿ-kap kiâⁿ

live in hum - ble fel - low - ship with our God.
khiam-pi kap Chú lí ê Sióng-tè saⁿ- kap kiâⁿ

42

This we can do for justice and for peace

Words: Brian Wren
Music: I-to Loh

1. This we can do for jus-tice and for peace: be
2. This we can do for jus-tice and for peace: reach

still, with time to pray, and heed the prayers that
out, and glad - ly give, that oth - ers too may

oth - er peo - ple say. This we can do, for
eat, and laugh, and live. This we can do, for

Christ has borne— the cross, re - veal - ing God, whose
Christ, with wine— and bread, brings food— and love to

gra - cious, win - ning love a -
sat - is - fy— us all, and—

- wakes a deep de - sire to— do what we can
lifts our thank - ful hearts to— do what we can

do, and see— it through.
do, and see— it through.

rit.

3. This we can do for justice and for peace:
sing out, and shed our fear,
when angry foes abuse and domineer.
This we can do, for Christ, unjustly killed,
arises over governments and powers,
and gives us peaceful strength
to do what we can do, and see it through.

4. This we can do for justice and for peace:
press on, and keep in view,
a dream of peace on earth, and all things new.
This we can do, for Christ, alive in God,
from God's tomorrow touches us with hope
and gives us faith renewed,
to do what we can do, and see it through.

Building a just society

BUNUNAR
adapt. I-to Loh & James Minchin

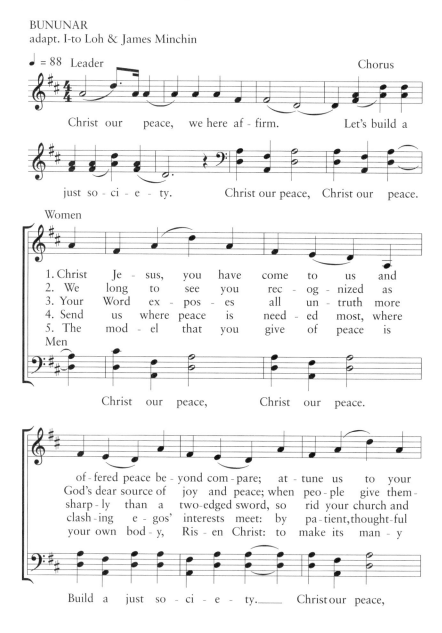

♩ = 88 Leader   Chorus

Christ our peace, we here af - firm. Let's build a

just so - ci - e - ty. Christ our peace, Christ our peace.

Women

1. Christ Je - sus, you have come to us and
2. We long to see you rec - og - nized as
3. Your Word ex - pos - es all un - truth more
4. Send us where peace is need - ed most, where
5. The mod - el that you give of peace is

Men

Christ our peace, Christ our peace.

of - fered peace be - yond com - pare; at - tune us to your
God's dear source of joy and peace; when peo - ple give them-
sharp - ly than a two-edged sword, so rid your church and
clash - ing e - gos' interests meet: by pa - tient, thought-ful
your own bod - y, Ris - en Christ: to make its man - y

Build a just so - ci - e - ty.___ Christ our peace,

46

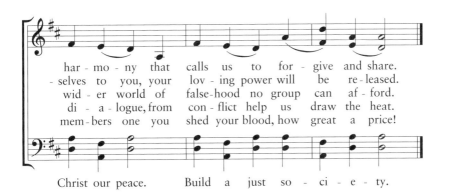

har - mo - ny that calls us to for - give and share.
- selves to you, your lov - ing power will be re - leased.
wid - er world of false-hood no group can af - ford.
di - a - logue, from con - flict help us draw the heat.
mem - bers one you shed your blood, how great a price!

Christ our peace. Build a just so - ci - e - ty.

From this time onwards

Bunun hymn tr. I-to Loh & James Minchin

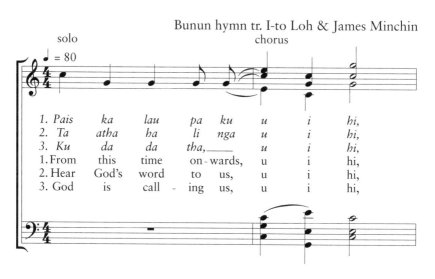

solo / chorus

♩ = 80

1. Pais ka lau pa ku u i hi,
2. Ta atha ha li nga u i hi,
3. Ku da da tha,____ u i hi,
1. From this time on-wards, u i hi,
2. Hear God's word to us, u i hi,
3. God is call - ing us, u i hi,

solo / chorus

mal ma na nu u i hi. Lis ka ta ma
min sial is ang u i hi. Ta hus du ma
mus kun Ta ma, u i hi. Ni tu ma tath,
let's strive hard - er, u i hi. Trust - ing Je - sus,
love each o - ther, u i hi. Walk to - geth - er,
'Look to Je - sus, u i hi, Death de - fy - ing,

u   i   hi,   ma dai dath tai-san u   i   hi.
u   i   hi,   min a   mu bu nun u   i   hi.
u   i   hi,   na sa   u ha - as, u   i   hi.
u   i   hi,   be - ing neigh-bour-ly. u   i   hi.
u   i   hi,   live in harm - o - ny. u   i   hi.
u   i   hi,   He's vic - tor - i-ous!' u   i   hi.

One family

Noel Dexter

Your skin co-lour is dif-ferent, Our foods are not the
same. Your clothes don't look like my clothes. You may not know my
name. Yet we are all Gods' child-ren, We're one big fam-i-
-ly ___ all made in our God's im-age in rich di-ver-si-

Chorus

- ty. We're all in one fam - i - ly, One fam - i - ly ____ are we. So let us all live to - ge - ther in peace and u - ni - ty.

You may live in the East side
While I live in the West
And you are busy working
While I am still at rest.
Yet we share the same sun
And one moon lights our night.
These are gifts from one Father,
The God of truth and light.

Chorus

God our Father, we thank you
For gifts so rich and free:
For love which still unites us
Wherever we may be.
In Christ we find our future,
Our destiny, our joy,
A foretaste of fulfilment
That nothing can destroy.

Chorus

Let justice be our guide

Words: Brian Wren and Arao Litsure   Music: Arao Litsure

Let jus-tice be our __ guide Lead us in your ways of

truth for __ ev - er __

la la, la la la da la __ la la la __

Eh Vukani (Hey, people of God)

Cantor: Eh Vukani vanhu va Jehova.
          (Hey, people of God, wake up.)
All: **Eh Vukani vanhu va Jehova.**

Cantor: Khozelani Jehova vanhu va Jehova.
          (Worship God, people of God.)
All: **Khozelani Jehova vanhu va Jehova.**

Cantor: Eh Vukani vanhu va Jehova.
All: **Eh Vukani vanhu va Jehova.**

Cantor: Khozelani Jehova vanhu va Jehova.
All: **Khozelani Jehova vanhu va Jehova.**

All: **Eh Vukani vanhu va Jehova.**
           Eh Vukani vanhu va Jehova.
           Eh Vukani vanhu va Jehova.
           Eh Vukani vanhu va Jehova.
           Eh Vukani vanhu va Jehova.

Arao Litsure

Eh Vukani

B

x2

Kho - ze - la - ni   Je - ho - va   va - nhu va Je - ho - va

D

Eh_____ Vu - ka - ni   va - nhu va Je - ho - va

Eh_____ Vu - ka - ni   va - nhu va Je - ho - va

Eh _____ Vu-ka – ni va-nhu va Je-ho – va

Eh _____ Vu-ka – ni va-nhu va Je-ho – va

Eh _____ Vu-ka – ni va-nhu va Je-ho – va

To break the chains

To go with the 'Fasting' litany, p. 72.

Kachin Melody (adapted) Words: Wesley Ariarajah & Brian Wren
Music: I-to Loh

Lead us in paths of truth

Words: Brian Wren
Music: I-to Loh

♩ = 84

Lead us in paths _____ of truth.

Let love our light _____ pro - vide. In

work or lei - sure, age _____ or _____ youth,

let jus - tice be our _____ guide.

Living in a world that suffers

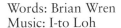

Words: Brian Wren
Music: I-to Loh

1. Liv - ing in a world that suf-fers,
2. In the grief, by fear un-daunt-ed,

pain and e - vil fret our mind. Rea - son ends with
tell - ing truth through tear - ful songs, in the burst of

brok - en an-swers. Let us pray, and
lov - ing ang - er, giv - ing strength to

hope ___ to find, through each oth - er, ___
tac - kle wrongs, in ___ a neigh-bour, ___

joined ___ to - geth - er, Christ ___ a - live, ___ car-ing,
in ___ a stran - ger, show ___ your love, liv-ing,

bear - ing e - vil, giv - ing joy that the
glow - ing, warm-ing, gleam - ing bright, like a

world can - not ___ des - troy.
can - dle in ___ the night.

Calls to Worship

Listen and look

Based on Psalm 82.

L = Leader. R = Response.

L: Listen and look:
the court is in session.
The God of Jesus Christ will judge the earth.

R: **What will you judge, Great Living God?**

L: Listen and look:
'The world is my courtroom,
and every power on earth shall answer me.'

R: **How will you judge, Great Living God?**

L: Listen and look:
the poor and the hungry
shall be my witnesses against you all.

R: **Hear and forgive, Great Living God!**

Brian Wren

For national occasions

One: Proclaim liberty throughout the land,
to all its inhabitants.

All: **Proclaim freedom, justice and peace,
to all who live on earth.**

One: Christ, who loves every nation,
is lifted up above all nations,
to draw the whole world together,
in freedom, justice and peace.

All: We are the body of Christ.
May we become a living sign
of all that God has done,
and all that God will do. Amen.

Brian Wren

Prayers

Gifts

Because you have blessed us
and have called us to serve you,
we come to you.

Because you have given us the earth to care for
but we take more than our share,
we come to you.

Because you have given so much
but we worship the gifts rather than the Giver,
we come to you.

Because you called us to love our neighbours
but we fail to see their needs,
we come to you.

Because you have given us food and clothes
but still we seek to possess more,
we come to you.

Because you are the God of love
and we need your grace,
we come to you.

Gracious God,
come to us and meet us on the way.
You have given generously
but we do not know how to respond.
So help us to strive for integrity and faithfulness,
love and gentleness,
purity and endurance,
that we may only and always serve you.

Francis Brienen

A prayer for Passiontide

Compassionate God,
we pray for those who have no land,
who work the fields of others,
who pick the fruit
but do not know its taste.

We pray for those who have no home,
who are displaced, uprooted,
their homes destroyed
by landlords and warlords.

We pray for those who have lost their children,
for whom there is no future,
their sons taken to war,
their daughters sold into slavery.

May their dreams be not broken,
May their spirits be not crushed,
May their lives be not forgotten.

Instead, break our dreams of 'more', O God,
and crush our spirit of greed,
we for whom enough is never enough,
who do not understand the tears of the poor,
whose way of life perpetuates the grip of suffering.

Christ who went before us,
help us to remember in your passion
all those who suffer.
Help us to remember in your passion
the promise of justice,
the promise of peace,
the promise of new life.
You who in your life on earth
cried out to God, pray for us now.

Francis Brienen

Treading down the evils

Let us remember God's promise:
'I shall pour out my Spirit on all humanity.'

Where truth is compromised
to serve the mighty and the powerful,
empower us to tread down untruthfulness.

Where community is broken down
in the pursuit of relentless personal ambition,
empower us to tread down selfishness.

Where barriers are created
for the glorification of race, gender, religion or tradition,
empower us to tread down division.

Where the poor are kept poor
and opportunity is taken away,
empower us to tread down exploitation.

Where the just are killed
and prophets are silenced,
empower us to tread down oppression.

Where nature is destroyed,
sold out as a mere commodity,
empower us to tread down blasphemy.

**Empower us, triune God,
to tread down the evils in our world.
Teach us your way of life,
fill us with the joy of your presence
and we will watch Satan fall.**

Francis Brienen

Confession

Read Luke 7:36–47

Voice 1: 'Do you see this woman?'

Voice 2: No! I only see a sinner.

Voice 1: Lord, forgive us when we fail to see people and only see problems.
Forgive us when we walk past on the other side.
Forgive us when we piously claim to hate the sin and love the sinner and yet are afraid to make contact with the sinners of this world.
Lord, in your mercy

All: **hear our prayer.**

Voice 1: 'Do you see this woman?'

Voice 2: No! I see an opportunity for a theological debate.

Voice 1: Lord, forgive us when we are so caught up with our own agenda, that we miss the cries of pain and hurt around us.
Forgive us when we would prefer to talk about problems rather than spend our time in loving service.
Forgive us when our talking takes so long that we run out of times for action.
Lord, in your mercy

All: **hear our prayer.**

Voice 1: 'Do you see this woman?'

Voice 2: No! I see a social problem.

Voice 1: Forgive us, Lord, when we are so overwhelmed by the enormity of problems that we fail to respond to individuals.
Forgive us when our excuse remains,
'I don't yet have enough information on which to act.'

Forgive us, God, when we think that people's problems are someone else's responsibility.
Lord, in your mercy

All: **hear our prayer.**

Voice 1: 'Do you see this woman?'

Voice 2: No! I see a label – this one is 'prostitute'.

Voice 1: Forgive us, Lord, when our labels, stereotypes and prejudices prevent us from relating to people.
Forgive us when we deem some people not worthy of our attention.
Forgive us, especially, that we are most unready to relate to the very people that you related to.
Lord, in your mercy

All: **hear our prayer.**

Voice 1: 'Do you see this woman?'

Voice 2: Yes, but I am not moved to compassion or action.

Voice 1: Forgive us, Lord, our hardness of heart.
Forgive our ability to analyse and perceive situations of injustice, but out unwillingness to change ourselves
or to let go of our vested interest.
Forgive the times when we have seen the people and their needs, but have felt too fatigued to respond.
Lord, in your mercy

All: **hear our prayer.**

Conclude by reading Luke 7:48

Andrew Williams

A guiding star

God of all time,
who makes all things new,
we bring before you the year now ending.
For life full and good,
for opportunities recognized and taken,
for love known and shared,
we thank you.

Where we have fallen short,
forgive us.
When we worry over what is past,
free us.

As we begin again
and take our first few steps into the future,
where nothing is safe and certain,
except you,
we ask for the courage of the wise men
who simply went and followed a star.
We ask for their wisdom,
in choosing to pursue the deepest truth,
not knowing where they would be led.

In the year to come, God of all time,
be our help and company.
Hold our hands as we journey onwards
and may your dream of shalom,
where all will be at peace,
be our guiding star.

Francis Brienen

An offering prayer

Holy God, we give you ourselves, captive and free,
shaped by forces beyond our control,
yet open to the power of your Spirit.
Through us, and our gifts, may others know
that when anyone is in Christ, there is a new creation,
and that the old way ends, and new life begins
for everyone.
Amen.

Brian Wren

Easter affirmation and prayer

Christ is risen. Death has lost its sting.
Let us live in hope, and confess our faith:
With Martha and Peter we confess:
You are the Christ,
Wisdom in weakness,
Word made flesh,
Offspring of God,
Crucified and Risen,
Life in the midst of death.

Let us pray:
For people facing death
through illness, accident, or natural disaster,
and for those who love them, grieve for them,
and care for them.
Risen Christ, hear our prayer,
and help us care.

For people facing death through hunger, poverty,
the burdens of debt and the balance of trade,
in _____.
Risen Christ, hear our prayer,
and help us care.

For people facing death in war,
and grieving for their loved ones,
in _____.
Risen Christ, hear our prayer,
and help us care.

For people HIV positive, or living with AIDS,
that they may find friendship, love, and hope.
Risen Christ, hear our prayer,
and help us care.

For people longing for life,
who face the death of hope,
through homelessness, poverty, unemployment,
discrimination and oppression,
or because they drink the bitter waters
of other people's hatred and scorn.
Risen Christ, hear our prayer,
and help us care.

With Martha and Peter we confess:
You are the Christ,
Wisdom in weakness,
Word made flesh,
Offspring of God,
Crucified and Risen,
Life in the midst of death.
By grace, through faith,
we will sit with the sufferers,
stand by the outcasts,
walk with the exploited,
and sing with the oppressed
in your name. Amen.

Brian Wren

Easter praise

Living God, with loving power
you raised Jesus from the dead.
> So we need not fear death,
> but will trust your love.

Living God, with loving power
you overturned the powers of this world
that crucified your Chosen One.
> So we need not fear them,
> but will follow the way of Christ,
> with peaceful hope and persistent love.

Living God, with loving power
you sent your Spirit to renew us.
> So we will praise you, and be your people,
> now and always.

Amen.

Brian Wren

Litanies

Fasting

(From Isaiah 58:3–9)

'Why do we fast, but you do not see?
Why humble ourselves, but you do not notice?'

'Look, you serve your own interest
on your fasting day,
and oppress all your workers . . .
and strike with your wicked fist.
Will you call this a fast,
a day acceptable to the Lord?'

(Sing 'To break the chains', p. 57.)

'Is not this the fast that I choose:
to loose the bonds of injustice,
to undo the thongs of the yoke,
to let the oppressed go free,
and to break every yoke?'

(Sing: 'To break the chains'.)

'Is it not to share your bread
with the hungry,
and bring the homeless poor
into your house;
when you see the naked, to cover them,
and not to hide yourself from
your own kin?'

(Sing 'To break the chains'.)

'Then your light shall break forth
like the dawn,
and your healing shall spring up quickly . . .
Then you shall call, and the Lord will answer;
you shall cry for help, and he will say,
"Here I am."'

(Sing 'To break the chains'.)

Wesley Ariarajah

Break forth together into singing!

From the book of Isaiah.

L = Leader. P = People.

L: Do not remember the former things,
    or consider the things of old.
    I am about to do a new thing;
    now it springs forth, do you not
    perceive it?   (43:18–19a)

P: **I will make a way in the wilderness
    and rivers in the desert.**   (43:19b)

L: For I will pour water on the thirsty land,
    and streams on the dry ground;
    I will pour my Spirit upon your descendants,
    and my blessing on your offspring.   (44:3)

P: **I have swept away your transgressions like a cloud,
    and your sins like mist;
    return to me,
    for I have redeemed you.**   (44:22)

L: Sing, O heavens, for the Lord has done it;
    shout, O depths of the earth;
    break forth into singing, O mountains,
    O forest, and every tree in it!   (44:23)

P: For the Lord has comforted his people,
and will have compassion
on his suffering ones.   (49:13b)

L: How beautiful upon the mountains
are the feet of the messenger who announces peace,
who brings good news, who announces salvation . . .   (52:7)

P: Break forth together into singing . . .
For the Lord has comforted his people . . .
The Lord has bared his holy arm before
the eyes of all the nations;
and all the ends of the earth shall see
the salvation of our God.   (52:9–10)

Wesley Ariarajah

The movement of the Spirit

(This litany may be used in full or in parts; the symbolic actions are
   optional)

*Action: Use long ribbons in a circling motion over the heads of the
congregation. The ribbons will generate movement and energy. If
worship is held outside you might be able to use a kite to the same
effect.*

Voice 1:

In the beginning when God created the heavens and the earth,
the earth was a formless void and darkness covered the face of the
deep, while a wind from God swept over the face of the waters.
(Genesis 1:1–2)

Prayer:

Eternal God, the author of life,
your Spirit swept over the waters
and brought life into being;
may the same Spirit energize our lives

that we discover again
the wonder of the gift of life.

Action: *People are asked to breathe heavily on to the back of their hand so they feel the breath. They are encouraged to notice the warmth of their breath and reflect on the breath/Spirit which gives life. If it is appropriate people could be asked to breathe on to another person's hand.*

Voice 2:

Then he said to me, 'Prophesy to the breath, prophesy, mortal, and say to the breath: Thus says the Lord God: "Come from the four winds, O breath, and breathe upon these slain, that they may live."' (Ezekiel 37:9)

Prayer:

Living God, when doubts threaten our faith,
despair destroys our hopes, and when hatred
and war turn the earth into a valley of bones,
send us your Spirit and renew our lives.

Action: *People rededicate themselves to the task of sharing the good news, perhaps by offering a symbol, picture or few words about the particular gift they have to share. They are then anointed with perfume, oil or water.*

Voice 3:

The Spirit of the Lord is upon me, because he has
anointed me to preach good news to the poor.
He has sent me to proclaim release to the captives
and recovery of sight to the blind, to let the oppressed go free,
to proclaim the year of the Lord's favour. (Luke 4:18–19)

Prayer:

> Loving God, where ignorance and prejudice have fractured
> our life in community,
> where injustice and oppression
> have broken the spirit of people,
> anoint us with the power of your Spirit,
> to announce the in-breaking of your sovereign rule
> over all of life.

Action: Create a 'dream catcher' (indigenous North American device like a circular net for catching good dreams and allowing nightmares to escape) into which the dreams and visions of the congregation are placed. You could use a woven basket or tray. These could be dreams for themselves, their community or the world. The dreams could be represented by symbols, written or drawn on paper, or modelled. These are placed in the dream catcher.

Voice 4:

> Peter said: 'No, this is what was spoken through the prophet Joel:
> "In the last days it will be, God declares,
> that I will pour out my Spirit upon all flesh,
> and your sons and your daughters shall prophesy,
> and your young men shall see visions,
> and your old men shall dream dreams.
> Even upon my slaves, both men and women, in those days
> I will pour out my Spirit; and they shall prophesy."'
> (Acts 2:16–18)

Prayer:

> Merciful God, who by your Spirit
> has called us into a fellowship of love,
> and has broken down the barriers
> that separate us into races, genders, classes and ethnic groups'
> teach us to celebrate Pentecost,
> our oneness in diversity.

Action: Give everyone a stone and remind them that stones can be used for creative purposes, e.g. building houses, and for destruction, e.g. as weapons. Encourage people to hold the stone tightly in their *hands, noticing its warmth the longer that they hold it. After a short time invite people to exchange their stone with someone else while saying a short phrase such as, 'Receive my stone as a sign that I will never harm you' or 'I give you this stone as a foundation stone of friendship'.* *

Voice 5:

I therefore, the prisoner in the Lord, beg you to lead a life
worthy of the calling to which you have been called . . .
making every effort to maintain the unity of the Spirit
in the bond of peace. (Ephesians 4:1,3)

Prayer:

Gracious God, who has called us into unity as the sign and proof
of the reconciliation and peace you offer to all peoples'
help us not to betray that trust through our divisions.
Draw us closer together,
that the world may believe
what you intend for your whole creation.

Action: *Paper chains are distributed among the congregation which people break symbolizing the freedom they have in Christ. Some chains are also placed around bowls of fruit. These too are broken and the fruit then distributed, symbolizing that we are now free to enjoy the fruit of the Spirit.*

Voice 6:

For freedom Christ has set us free.
Stand firm, therefore, and do not submit again to a yoke of
slavery.
Live by the Spirit, I say, and do not gratify the desires of the flesh.
By contrast, the fruit of the Spirit is love, joy, peace, patience,
kindness, generosity, faithfulness, gentleness and self-control.
There is no law against such things.
If we live by the Spirit, let us also be guided by the Spirit.
(Galatians 5:1,16,22–23,25)

*This idea is based upon a symbolic action that took place during worship at the Second European Ecumenical Assembly in Graz, Austria, in 1997.

Prayer:

O God of life and light,
by the power of your Holy Spirit
remove the blindness
that the possessions of the earth
brings into our lives.
Teach us to see beyond what is seen.
And help us to drink from the fountain of your goodness
that we may walk in the light of life.
Amen.

Wesley Ariarajah & Lindsey Sanderson

Symbolic Acts

Loving God

From Deuteronomy 6.

Leader: The book of Deuteronomy sets out many of the commandments by which the ancient Hebrew people were to live.

Reader: Hear, O Israel: The LORD is our God, the LORD alone. You shall love the LORD your God with all your heart, and with all your soul, and with all your might. Keep these words that I am commanding you today in your heart. Recite them to your children and talk about them when you are at home and when you are away, when you lie down and when you rise. Bind them as a sign on your hand, fix them as an emblem on your forehead, and write them on the doorposts of your house and on your gates.

(Deuteronomy 6:4–9 NRSV)

Leader: Jesus called the words we have just heard 'the greatest commandment'. We are reminded that loving God is something which involves our whole being and takes place wherever we are – at home, at work, at school, with friends, on Sundays and every day of the week. It was so important to love God that the ancient Hebrew people were instructed to write the words on their houses and gates and attach the words to their hands and foreheads so they would not forget them.

Today we are remembering how important it is to love God. As a sign that we love God and try each day to love God in all the things we do, help each other to tie the piece of wool you have been given around your wrist. For the rest of today, in everything you do, the bracelet will remind you of the commandment to love God.

(The people tie on their bracelets.)

All: Loving God,
          because you first loved us,
          we reach out in love to you.
          Forgive us when we forget your love for us,
          Give us courage when loving you is difficult,
          Help us each day to learn more about your love,
          and to share it with the people we meet.
          Amen.

Lindsey Sanderson

Come, Holy Spirit

Introduction by worship leader:

The church celebrates the coming of the Holy Spirit on the Day of Pentecost, but references to God's Spirit are found throughout the Bible. Some of the most vivid descriptions are found in Wisdom of Solomon, a book found in the Apocrypha. The writer of the Wisdom of Solomon is lavish in his praise of wisdom whom he describes as

> a spirit that is intelligent and holy, unique in its kind yet made up of many parts, subtle, free moving, lucid, spotless, clear, neither harmed nor harming, loving what is good, eager, unhampered, beneficent, kindly towards mortals, steadfast, unerring, untouched by care, all-powerful, all-surveying, and permeating every intelligent, pure and most subtle spirit.
>
> (Wisdom of Solomon 7: 22–23, REB)

The writer also describes wisdom, the Spirit, as a fine mist who rises from the power of God (Wisdom of Solomon 7: 25, REB). As we join in singing a song about the Holy Spirit (or listen to music) you will feel the mist of the Spirit come upon you.

People are then invited to sing an appropriate song or listen to music. As they do so the congregation is sprayed with lightly perfumed water. A plant spray is ideal. This should be done from above the congregation if possible, even if this is just done by people with the sprays walking amongst the congregation as they sit and sing.

Songs that could be sung include: 'Send out your Spirit' by Brian Wren and Simei Monteiro sung as a meditative chant (see p. 181); 'Loving Spirit' by Shirley Murray and David Dell (*Drawn to the Wonder*; *Rejoice and Sing*; *Alleluia Aotearoa*); 'Oh let the power fall on me' by Birchfield Aymer (*Drawn to the Wonder*).

After the song or music the following prayer is said together:

Holy Spirit,
as you have fallen gently upon us,
settle as a fine mist upon your church.
Make her an instrument of your peace and justice,
of your love and hope,
of your joy and blessing.
Amen.

Lindsey Sanderson

Forgiveness and reconciliation

This symbolic action starts with various readings in different voices.

Voice 1:

Then Peter came and said to him, 'Lord, if another member of the church sins against me, how often should I forgive? As many as seven times?' Jesus said to him, 'Not seven times, but, I tell you, seventy-seven times.' (Matthew 18:21–22)

Voice 2:

And forgive us our debts, as we also have forgiven our debtors. (Matthew 6:12)

Voice 3:

You have heard that it was said, 'You shall love your neighbour and hate your enemy.' But I say to you, 'Love your enemies and pray for those who persecute you, so that you may be children of your Father in heaven; for he makes his sun rise on the evil and on the good, and sends rain on the righteous and on the unrighteous.' (Matthew 5:43–45)

Voice 4:

For if you forgive others their trespasses, your heavenly Father will also forgive you; but if you do not forgive others, neither will your Father forgive your trespasses. (Matthew 6:14–15)

After the readings members of the congregation or the group are given a small piece of paper and a pen or pencil. Everyone is invited to write down the name of someone who has done them harm and whom they cannot forgive. The pieces of paper are folded up. Prayers for forgiveness are then said. After the prayers people are invited to come forward and place their piece of paper in a tin container. The leader then burns the papers in the presence of the congregation as a symbol of forgiveness. The symbolic burning of the pieces of paper can be followed by further readings, such as Philippians 3:13, Psalm 103:8–13 or Psalm 145:8–9.

Cathy Bott

Complete Liturgies

A service of word and table

This liturgy comes from a Reformed tradition, informed by theological insights from Asia and Latin America. The communion order is a development of the Brighthelm Liturgy, prepared jointly with Revd Elizabeth A. S. King in October 1987, for Brighthelm United Reformed Church, Brighton, Sussex, England.

There are two leaders (celebrants), called 'One' and 'Another', who should be of different age and gender, so that no one person is misconstrued as the icon of Christ. Because Christ is present in the community gathered round the table, the congregation has spoken participation in the prayers, especially the Great Thanksgiving.

Words in plain type are spoken by celebrants/leaders; words in bold type are said by the congregation ('People') or everyone ('All'). The sign * means 'Please stand if able.'

The service of the word

*Call to worship

One: Our Creator calls us.
Our Saviour leads us.
The Spirit unites us.

All: **We come with thanksgiving and praise.**

One: In Wisdom God gave birth to all things,
loving and cherishing the earth.

All: **We will care for God's earth
and rejoice in its abundant life.**

One: In Christ, God loves and saves us.

All: We will tell the story of God's love,
and meet the living Word.

One: The Spirit calls us from hiding into wholeness,
from separation into unity,
from mistrust into love.

All: We will worship and work together,
in friendship, peace and love.

*Hymn

Prayer of approach

(Said by all, or by a worship leader.)

Holy and Loving God,
whose Spirit searches all creation,
you know what we hide, and what is hidden from us.
Come among us, that we may meet you,
and be touched and turned about,
healed, restored and renewed,
through Christ, our Friend and Saviour.

Scripture – First Testament

Hymn or Psalm

Scripture – Second Testament

Sermon

(Then one of the following, perhaps in rotation through the month: Affirmation of Faith; Thanksgiving; Lament and Confession of Trust; or Confession of Sin and Assurance of Pardon. For example:)

Confession of our sin and need of God

One: We are the body of Christ,
needing forgiveness and transformation.
Let us therefore confess our sin,
in the presence of God.

All: Holy and Loving God, we confess that we have sinned,
by choice, and by conditioning,
in ignorance, and in awareness,
on our own, and with others.
We take responsibility, and ask forgiveness.
By your Spirit, turn us from evil to good,
and give us time for amendment of life.
Help us to live truthfully,
And to practise justice, kindness, and faithfulness,
through Jesus Christ our Saviour. Amen.

(And/or:)

Christ among us, Partner and Saviour,
deliver us from the powers that kill body and spirit.
Give us new heart, new hope, and a new song.
Ease our tiredness, hold us in our pain and hurt,
and bring us from brokenness to wholeness,
by your power and in your name. Amen.

Assurance of pardon and new life

One: Receive and believe God's promise:
'Jesus Christ came into the world to save sinners';
'I will never leave you nor forsake you.'
Brothers and sisters in Christ, here is good news:
God loves and values us, and forgives what is past.
In Christ God reaches out to heal and renew us.
Trust in your heart the promise of new life,
and proclaim with your lips the goodness of God:

Sung acclamation

Hymn

Prayers of the people

(For example, this prayer:)

Another: Let us pray.
Holy God, maker and mother of all,
you grieve when your children hurt each other,
defending the weak with fierce love,

and calling the strong to account.
Help us, and hear our prayer.

For all who suffer at the hands of others:
for children and adults abused, or recovering from abuse,
for people hurt in their closest relationships,
for people tortured, held hostage or unjustly imprisoned,
> let there be someone who listens,
> **All: And let their cry be heard.**

Another: For nations and peoples under domination,
trapped in poverty and debt,
or colonized in mind and spirit,
and for nations and peoples at war,
> let there be someone who listens,
> **All: And let their cry be heard.**

Another: For people scorned, scapegoated, or oppressed
because of their gender, colour,
their sexual orientation,
their age or their appearance,
their condition of mind and body,
or any other cause . . .
> let there be someone who listens,
> **All: And let their cry be heard.**

Another: For people in pain and grief,
in loneliness and emptiness,
in shame and remorse,
> let there be someone who listens,
> **All: And let their cry be heard.**

Another: For people and needs that we name before you
in silence, or in speech . . . *(pause)* . . .
> let there be someone who listens,
> **All: And let their cry be heard.**

Another: There is a balm in Gilead,
to make the wounded whole.
There is a balm in Gilead,
to heal the sin-sick soul.

In every insult, rift and war,
where colour, scorn or wealth divide,
Christ suffers still, and loves the more,
and lives, where even hope has died.
This is our faith. Let us live in faith,
trusting that God will make all things new,
through Jesus Christ, in whose name we pray. **Amen.**

*The peace

One: At peace with God, we are reconciled to each other.
The peace of God be always with you.

All: **And also with you.**
(Greetings of peace in Christ are exchanged.)

The service of the table

One: In Christ, God invites us, saying:

Another: 'Come to me, all who labour and are heavy laden,
and I will give you rest.'

One: 'I am the bread of life.
Whoever comes to me shall never be hungry.
Whoever trusts in me shall never be thirsty.'

Another: 'Whoever comes to me
I will never turn away.'

*Hymn

The offering

*(Bread and wine are brought to the table, with a money offering, if taken. *A Doxology may be sung, e.g.:)*

**Praise God, the Giver and the Gift.
Hearts, minds and voices now uplift:
Alleluia! Alleluia!**

Praise, praise the Breath of glad surprise,
freeing, uplifting, op'ning eyes,
    Three-in-Oneness, Love communing,
    Alleluia! Alleluia! Alleluia!

*Words © Hope Publishing Company for USA, Canada, Australia and New
Zealand; © Stainer and Bell for all other territories.
Tune: 'LASST UNS ERFREUEN'.*

Declaration and dedication

*(The words in square brackets are used if a money offering is
received.)*

[One: To the table of Christ we bring money,
            gained by using God's gifts,
            and we give ourselves
            to be Christ's body in the world.]

[**All:**   **We offer ourselves to serve Jesus Christ
            in love, justice and peace.]**

One: To the table of Christ we bring bread and wine,
            made by people's work in an unjust world
            where some have plenty, and most go hungry,
            some are applauded, and many despised.

All: **At this table everyone is fed, and no one has to pay;
            everyone shares the cup of pain and celebration;
            everyone is honoured, and no one is despised.**

Another: This bread and wine shall be our communion
            in the body and blood of Christ:

All: **our constitution as Christ's new community,
            our protest against poverty and hunger,
            and our sign of hope for a new world,
            where God is praised, every life is valued,
            and every child is fed.**

*The Great Thanksgiving

(The congregation may sit or kneel throughout, or stand until the Sanctus ('Holy, Holy, Holy'), according to local custom.)

One: Lift up your hearts!

People: **We lift our hearts to the living God.**

Another: Let us give thanks to God.

People: **It is right, and always right,**
          with body, mind and spirit,
          to bring to God our thanks and praise.

Another: We thank you and praise you,
          giver of life and lover of creation,
          for creating and bringing to birth
          this unfathomed universe of space and time,
          with stars and planets, and our own good earth.

People: **We thank you that we are not alone,**
          but part of earth's living body,
          outcome of untold generations,
          and offspring of your love.

Another: We thank you for creating us to know and love you,
          and for bringing us into the body of Christ,
          that we may sing and tell your goodness,
          replenish the earth, and make peace and justice.

All: **You fill us with worth, call us to account,**
          and promise us eternal life.

Another: Therefore with all your people,
          past, present, and to come,
          and with all the company of heaven,
          we praise your name, in joy and wonder:

All: Holy, Holy, Holy God,
love's empowering might,
heaven and earth are full of your glory.
Hosanna in the highest!
Blessed is the One who comes in the name of God.
Hosanna in the highest!

One: We thank you for Jesus, your Anointed One,
born of a woman, Word made flesh,
in whom we fully know your goodness and love.

All: We thank you for this unforgettable person
who showed us what life is meant to be,
reaching out in costly, unexpected love.
We remember his birth and growth,
his teaching and healing,
his love for women, children and men,
his ministry in Galilee and Jerusalem,
his death on the cross, and his resurrection in glory.

One: We praise you as we remember
that on the night when he was betrayed
to the governing authorities,
he had a meal with his disciples.

All: We remember with thanks, that as they sat at table,
Jesus took bread and a wine-cup, saying:

One: 'This is my body, given for you.
Do this in remembrance of me.'

Another: 'This cup is the new covenant,
sealed by my blood.
Do this, as often as you drink it,
in remembrance of me.'

One: We remember with thanks, that in taking bread and cup,
Jesus lifted up the history of his people,
foresaw his own suffering and death,
and prophesied that God would bring from it
freedom, hope and life.

All: **Christ our Passover is sacrificed for us.**
        Therefore let us keep the feast.

Another: We praise you,
        that when Christ's body was unjustly broken,
        and his life poured out in suffering and death,
        you raised him up, and poured out your Spirit,
        on Gentile and Jew, women and men,
        old and young, slave and free.

All: **By the presence of your Spirit,**
        give us life and love in Christ
        as we share this bread and wine.

One: May the Spirit bring justice and peace
        to all living things, and all earth's people
        as we wait in hope
        for the feast of eternal homecoming,
        and offer our sacrifice of praise:

All: **Christ has died.**
        Christ is risen.
        Christ will come again.

One: Holy and loving God,
        Source, Guide and Goal of all that is,
        to you be all honour and glory,
        with Jesus Christ, in the unity of the Holy Spirit,
        now and for ever.

All: **Amen!**

One: As Jesus taught his disciples, so now we pray:
        (Alternative wording in italics.)

All: **Our Father in heaven,**
        hallowed be your name,
        your kingdom come,
        (may your sovereignty come)
        your will be done,
        on earth as in heaven.

Give us today our daily bread,
and forgive us our sins,
(and forgive our debts)
as we forgive those who sin against us.
(as we forgive our debtors)
Save us from the time of trial,
(Save us from temptation,)
and deliver us from evil.
For the kingdom, and the power,
(For the sovereignty, and the power,)
and the glory are yours,
now and for ever. Amen.

Breaking the bread and lifting the cup

Another: The bread we break *(breaking the bread)*
is our communion in the body of Christ.

One: The cup we bless *(lifting the cup)*
is our communion in the blood of Christ.

Another: The gifts of God for the people of God.
Come, all is ready.
(Communion follows, according to local custom.)

Prayer after communion

One: Let us pray . . . Holy and loving God,
we praise you for inviting us to this table,
for all you give, and for all you promise.

All: Help us to go out from this place,
at peace with you, with ourselves, and with each other,
to do justice, love kindness,
and walk humbly with you, our God,
through Christ our Saviour,
to whom, with you and the Holy Spirit, One God,
be glory and praise, now and for ever. Amen.

*Hymn

Dismissal with blessing

Another: May the Giver of Law, the Word of Grace,
and the Breath of Life, One God,
help us to love justice, trust love,
and live faithfully,
through Christ, our joy and Saviour.

People: **Amen.**

One: Go in peace, rejoicing in the power of the Holy Spirit.

People: **Thanks be to God!**

Brian Wren

Part 3

Loving Service

Hymns and Songs

The washing of the feet

Words & music: Jaci C Maraschin
Translation: Brian Wren

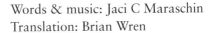

pés, hu - mil - de - men - te,_____ en -
ser - vant washed their dirty feet, you

vias te-os, lo - go a - pós, en - tre os pe - ri - gos_____
sent then to a world that would not understand,_____

de um mun - do de - su - ma-no e in-co - e -
through dan - ger as your mes - sen - gers to

96

RPm

ren - te._____

2. You

ev - ery land.

You will not let us hide within a holy place,
but send us out to demonstrate your healing grace,
to follow your example and to wash the feet
of travellers and sufferers we chance to meet.

As on the dusty road of life we walk with you,
come, wash our aching feet again, and give anew
the joyful love that, in a world so pitiless,
can bind the wounds of weariness and deep distress.

Come Jesus, wash our hearts and give us, deep within,
the joy of hope reborn, and of forgiven sin,
as with the dancing feet of heaven's messengers
we speak about your love, and sing your promises.

Jesus Christ sets free to serve

Words: CCA

Music: SEOUL, I-to Loh

If we love one another

I John 4:12   Music: I-to Loh

No one - has ev - er seen_____ God, no
Chiông - lâi bē ū lâng khòaⁿ - kī Siòng-tè, chiông

one has ev - er seen_____ God, if we love one an-o-ther,
lâi bē ū lâng khòaⁿ-kī Siòng-tè, Lán tāi ke nā ū saⁿ-thiàⁿ,

love one an-o-ther, God lives in us, and God's
lán nā ū saⁿ-thiàⁿ, Siòng - tè chiū-tiàm tī lán,

love is per-fect - ed in us, and God's
I ê thiàⁿ oân - choân tī lán, iā

love   is per - fect - ed in   us.
I   ê thià oân - choân tī lán.

Christ's freedom meal

Music: Brian Wren
Music: I-to Loh

When be - liev - ers break the bread,
When a stran - ger's not a - lone,

when a hun - gry child is fed,
where the home - less find a home,

praise the love that Christ___ re - vealed,___
praise the love that Christ___ re - vealed,___

liv-ing,   work-ing_____ in____ our__ world.
liv-ing,   work-ing_____ in____ our__ world.

Guaicuru Kyrie

A kyrie from the Guaicuru, a native people of Brazil.

Words and music: Simei Monteiro

Ou - ve, Deus de'a - mor, nos - so cla - mor!
¡O - ye, Dios de'a - mor, nues - tro cla - mor!
Hear, __ God of love, our cry to you!

Ou - ve, Deus de'a - mor, nos - so cla - mor!
¡O - ye, Dios de'a - mor, nues - tro cla - mor!
Hear, __ God of love, our cry to you!

Ou - ve, Deus de'a - mor, ou - ve, Deus de'a - mor,
O - ye, Dios de'a - mor, o - ye, Dios de'a - mor,
Hear, __ God of love, hear, __ God of love,

ou - ve, Deus de'a - mor, ou - ve Deus de'a - mor,
o - ye, Dios de'a - mor, o - ye, Dios de'a - mor,
hear, __ God of love, hear, __ God of loves

o nos - so cla - mor, o nos - so cla - mor.
el nues - tro cla - mor, el nues - tro cla - mor.
our___ cry to you, our cry___ to you.

Ou - ve, Deus de'a - mor, ___ nos - so cla - mor!
¡O - ye, Dios de'a - mor, ___ nues - tro cla - mor!
Hear,___ God of love, ___ our cry to you!

Loku famba/Look around you

This song can be used as a call to worship or a prayer response.

Arao Litsure

Lo-ku fa- mba we-tchu wu-ka nza ko U-ta
wo-na va ku ra nza ko Na-we-na-wu ra-nza la vo
ta-la U-ta ku-ma a ku ha-nyi-swa

Translation: (not for singing)
    When walking, look around you,
    You will see people who love you.
    You must also love others,
    You will be saved.

A Christmas Hymn

Music: Traditional   Words: Andrew Williams

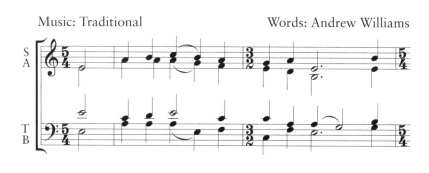

1. O, sing of God's outrageous grace
   Who greets us in a child's face.
   Our God divinity denies
   To see the world through human eyes.

106

2. So God to us in human guise
   Comes near salvation to devise.
   That Christ was born in poverty
   Shows God in all humility.

3. So angels sing and stones cry out,
   The earth itself takes up the shout,
   'Glory to God, on earth be peace'
   And those held captive find release.

4. If God is born then hope is true
   And human flesh refashioned, new.
   Dare we like him be re-made poor
   And lose ourselves by loving more?

5. For we have human eyes to see
   The same world in its misery.
   Will we like God share in this pain
   Or choosing heaven, there remain?

Calls to Worship

We are the hands of Christ

Based on Romans 12:4–21.

L = Leader. R = Response.

L: We are the hands of Christ.
R: Fill us with kindness.
L: We are the feet of Christ.
R: Speed us with joy.
L: We are the eyes of Christ,
R: seeing as Christ sees.
L: We are the lips of Christ,
R: speaking with love.
L: We are the ears of Christ,
R: ready to listen.
L: We are the arms of Christ,
R: serving with love.

Brian Wren

Prayers

A litany of intercession

To be used at All Saints and at other times. Words in bold can be spoken as a response by all.

Two: Living God, fountain of life, flowing with love,
in Christ you give us living water.
By your Spirit we are washed, refreshed, and renewed.
In prayer, we reach out to the world,
thirsting for justice, peace, and kindness.

One: For all who are meeting here,
that our purposes may find your purpose,
and be led by your wisdom and love,
we pray in hope, **and join our love with yours.**

Two: For the church, local and universal,
that your Spirit may bring us close to Christ,
and closer to each other,
we pray in hope, **and join our love with yours.**

One: For people in need,
through hunger, illness, imprisonment,
abuse, oppression, and war,
that the Spirit of Christ may restrain wrongdoers,
and bring comfort to mourners,
persistence to peacemakers,
and courage to all who thirst for what is right,
we pray in hope, **and join our love with yours.**

Two: For this nation,
and all who have power and influence within it,
in politics, business, the media, culture and religion,
that we may seek and cherish

justice, freedom, tranquillity, and dignity for all,
we pray in hope, **and join our love with yours.**

One: For all the nations and peoples,
that we may grow together in humility, respect, and care
for all human beings, and for all living things,
we pray in hope, **and join our love with yours.**

Two: For people with faiths other than our own,
that as we sing and tell our Saviour's story,
we may listen to their stories,
and find wisdom, hope, and truth,
we pray in hope, **and join our love with yours.**

One: For all saints, ordinary or famous,
living on earth, or alive in you,
we give thanks, and pray that,
as your saints sustain us,
so we may sustain others.
We pray in hope, **and join our love with yours.**

Two: Living God, Living Christ, Living Spirit,
to you belong all worship, thanksgiving, and praise.
Accept our love, and lead us on,
reborn, refreshed, and renewed,
through Christ,
our Rescuer, Companion and Friend. Amen.

Brian Wren

Christ, you meet us

*Call and Response: The congregation responds with the same
text and melody.*

Words: Brian Wren
Music: I-to Loh

1. Christ, you meet ____ us where - ev - er we go.
3. Love _ and wis - dom we glad - ly re - ceive.
4. From _ the neigh - bours we're kneel - ing to serve.
5. Come _ and meet ____ us, where - ev - er we go.

2. Where-ev - er we go you have al - ways been there.
6. Where-ev - er we go you will al - ways be there.

I will follow you wherever you go

Christ, you are calling.
In the poor,
in the sick,
in the hungry,
in the dying,
you are waiting for me.

Christ, you are calling.
In the hated,
in the hopeless,
in the helpless,
in the haunted,
you are waiting for me.

Christ, you are calling.
In the homeless,
in the stranger,
in the children,
in me,
you are waiting for me.

I want to follow you, Christ Jesus,
so when you call,
help me to hear your voice.
When you beckon,
help me not to look back.
In the face of the unfamiliar
strengthen my commitment
and make me fit for your kingdom.

Francis Brienen

The word made flesh

Christ Jesus, full of grace and truth,
you lived among us,
as a man of your people
and a man of your time.

You are the word made flesh.

When many distance themselves from the church,
help us to see that it may be
because the church has stopped being with the people,
because it has sought to be on good terms with the powerful.

Help your church to know that it can serve best
when it does not set itself apart,
when it feels as its own all that is human,
when it suffers with those who weep,
when it is happy with those who rejoice
and when it welcomes sinners.

Christ Jesus, full of grace and truth,
you are the word made flesh.
May the church serve in your likeness,
may it bring light in the darkness,
may it bring hope to those who have lost faith,
may it walk in your footsteps,
may it be love in deed.

**Christ Jesus,
continue to become incarnate in all of us.**

Francis Brienen

Prayer of intercession

This prayer can be said while using visual aids such as slides or large photographs. The words of the prayer are on the left, the images that correspond with the words on the right. After each section of the prayer the chorus 'O Lord, hear our cry' is sung.

This prayer requires some preparation. You will need to collect slides, photographs or newspaper images. Please note that the images described below are suggestions only. Some adaptation to your own context will be necessary.

Words	*Image*
Let us pray for our world	*Earth from outer space*
A world so fractured by hate	*Tank/soldiers*
Disasters we cannot control	*Drought/flood*
But where our actions can make a difference	*Happy children*
Let us consider how we contribute to people's pain	*Man/Woman in distress*
By our actions	*Bombed house or building*
And our neglect	*People begging for food*
Let us pray for our war torn world	*Bombs/war scenes*
And especially for the children who have lived all their days in the midst of violence	*Image of children in war torn area*
And poverty	*Image of children in poverty*
And hunger	*Baby crying*

O Lord, hear our cry, O Lord, hear our prayer

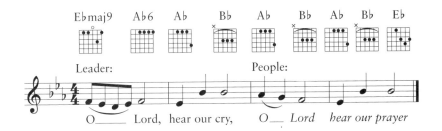

Leader: O___ Lord, hear our cry,　People: O__ Lord hear our prayer

Let us pray for the communities where we live	*Rural scene/city landscape*
For those whose work is drudgery	*Factory workers*
For those who feel they receive an unfair reward for their work	*Farmers' fields*
And for those who have no work	*Graffiti on wall*
For those who cannot forget old hurts	*War graves/war memorial*
For those condemned to the fringes of society	*An excluded group in your society*
For those whose pain is swallowed in the joy of new beginnings	*Birth of a baby*
And for the children of our community Well fed	*Children eating*
Well-educated	*Classroom scene*
And yet vulnerable, in need of care	*Child in tears*

O Lord, hear our cry, O Lord, hear our prayer

Let us pray for the church	*Multi-ethnic group*
The church which God loves	*Cross*
And for which Christ died	*Crucifix*
Let us pray for God's people	*Hands*
That we might be a rainbow people of promise	*Rainbow*
That we might be a people of hope	*Hands in the air*
Who instil hope in others	*Children playing*
Who provide a place of refuge	*Child's hand in adult's hand*
A place to belong	*Your congregation*
A place to love	*Group of friends/family*

O Lord, hear our cry, O Lord, hear our prayer.

Andrew Williams

Closing prayer

Sending God,
    You call each one of us to share in your mission,
    To proclaim,
    To nurture,
    To love,
    To transform,
    To renew.

Help us to be faithful to your calling.
Give us wisdom and insight to discern your voice.
Give us patience and humility to work with others.
Give us courage and strength when we feel overwhelmed
by the task before us.

Remind us of your presence with us.
Surround us with your all-embracing love.
Fill us with the joy and energy of your Spirit.
Prompt us to recall the example of Jesus.

And as you now send us out,
Back to our homes and families,
Our business and our leisure,
Keep us close to you,
This day and for ever more.
Amen.

Lindsey Sanderson

Symbolic Acts

The circle of love

This activity can be used by a group (youth or adult) or by a congregation in worship.

The basic idea

A group meets in a circle, to worship, and care for each other. They start reading 1 Corinthians 13 (NRSV) – from Bibles, or from the printed script below (page 122). But others want to join them – so whenever someone asks to join them, they have to stop reading, make a space for the newcomer(s), and welcome them, before they can carry on with their worship. The people who begin are called Starters. The others are Joiners. To find out who is who, cards are handed out. Those with the word 'Starter' form the Starter circle. The others have keywords from 1 Corinthians 13 (see below).

When they hear their word read aloud, they raise their hand(s). One or more people get a card labelled 'Greeter' – they are given a bell or chime, which they ring the moment they see a hand go up. The Greeters are in the Starter circle, not reading but facing outwards, watching for Joiners. When the bell rings, the Starter circle stops reading, greets the newcomer(s), gives them a copy of the scripture reading, and continues. The circle is complete when everyone has joined it.

Planning and action – for a group activity

Needs

- A room of adequate size.
- A circle of chairs in the centre – enough for the Starters and Greeter(s) (see below).

- Portable chairs for everyone else, in a larger circle about ten to fifteen feet out from the Starter circle.
- Word-cards for everyone (use the lists below as a guide).
- Enough NRSV Bibles or copies of 1 Corinthians 13 (from the script below) for everyone.

Action

Set out the chairs, give out the cards, and ask the Starters and Greeters to assemble in their circle. Explain that the Starters and Greeters are a group who are meeting to worship and pray together, and that they will welcome anyone who joins them. Then brief the two groups as follows.

Starters and Greeters

When their action starts, begin reading the passage aloud, going round the group, one sentence each. When someone raises their hand, the Greeters ring the bell, and the scripture reading stops. Then:

- Add a chair, widen the circle.
- Say a word of welcome (e.g. 'Yes, of course' or 'Welcome to the circle').
- Give them a Bible or script.
- Help them find their place.
- Invite one of them to start reading aloud at the beginning of the sentence you were in.

Important note: Read clearly and slowly, and speak up (to give the listeners a chance).

Joiners

Listen carefully for your code word (the one on your card). When you hear it:

- Raise your hand, and when the bell rings, call out that you want to join in.
- The group will make you welcome and show you what to do.
- When others want to join, make them welcome also.

Important note: Read clearly and slowly, and speak up (to give the listeners a chance).

Planning and action – for a congregation

Needs

- Enough space at a central or focal point, visible to all, for the Starters and Greeters to form their circle, standing together.
- Microphone(s) so that the readers can be heard by all. A hand mike is OK, if passed from reader to reader.
- Word-cards for everyone (use the lists below as a guide).
- Enough NRSV Bibles or copies of 1 Corinthians 13 (from the script below) for everyone.

Action

- Give out the cards as people come into worship – ushers should explain that they'll be needed, so please keep them handy. Worship leaders repeat this at the beginning of worship. In most congregations it will be best to select the Starters and Greeters beforehand, from people who will be happy and able to do this.
- When children are present, be sure to give them and their accompanying adult or older child the same cards, so that they stay together, and the older can help the younger.
- At the appropriate time, ask everyone to look at their card, and invite the Starters and Greeters to assemble in their circle. Explain that the Starters and Greeters are a group who are meeting to worship and pray together, and that they will welcome anyone who joins them. Then brief the two groups, as follows.

Starters and Greeters

When the action starts, begin reading the passage aloud, going round the group, one sentence each. Help each other by holding and passing the microphone, so that the readers are easily heard by all the congregation. Whenever someone raises their hand, the Greeters ring the bell, and the scripture reading stops. Then:

- Turn round, widen the circle, and welcome the new arrival(s).
- Give them a Bible or script, and help them find their place.
- Invite one of them to start reading aloud at the beginning of the sentence you were in.

Important note: Read clearly and slowly, and speak up (to give the listeners a chance).

Joiners

Listen carefully for your code word (the one on your card). When you hear it:

- Immediately raise your hand, and when the bell rings, call out that you want to join in.
- The group will make you welcome and show you what to do.
- When others want to join, make them welcome also.
- If you miss your code word, raise your hand when you hear the words 'face to face'.

Important note: When you are in the circle, read clearly and slowly, and speak up (to give the listeners a chance).

Afterwards

When everyone is in the circle, and the group has finished reading 1 Corinthians 13, try one or more of the following options:

- Have someone, or everyone, read 1 Corinthians 13 aloud.
- Ask each person to find two others, and share how they felt about the experience, and what it meant to them (time: four to six minutes). Then invite some to share what the experience meant for them, or said to them (offer the microphone if the activity is being done in the congregation). Let people go back to their seats if they've been standing for a while.
- Ask people to give each other greetings and signs of peace (e.g. 'Peace be with you').
- Offer a short prayer.
- Sing an appropriate hymn or song that everyone knows well.
- Offer the following suggestions for thought (but only if no one else has already made comments along these lines):

The chapter you were reading is about love. Love welcomes and includes people. By letting people join the circle, you were showing love to them. Widening the circle means starting over, and interrupting what you were doing; but that's how you include more people. The circle is full, but not complete. Add one empty chair (if in a small group) or think of the world out there (if in a congregation). A church or group should be an open circle of love.

The cards

How many cards?

An approximate guide:

	Number of people			
	12	20	40	50+
Greeter	1	2	3	4
Starter	4	6	7	8
Angels	1	1	1	1
Mysteries	1	1	1	1
Faith	1	1	2	2
Patient	1	1	2	3
Rejoice	1	1	3	4
Truth	1	1	3	5
Love never ends	1	2	4	9
Child	0	2	6	12
Face to face	0	2	8	all the rest

Tips

- Index cards are suitable.
- Make enough cards beforehand for the maximum probable numbers expected.
- Make two packs of cards: Pack 1 includes the Starters and Greeters, plus one each of the others; Pack 2 has the remainder.
- Shuffle both packs, and give out Pack 1 first, so that you are sure to have Starters, Greeters and enough Joiners to play the game.
- When making the cards, use lower-case lettering; it is easier to read than CAPITALS.
- Make the cards look inviting and colourful.

1 Corinthians 13 – (NRSV)

Read slowly and clearly, one phrase or sentence each:

If I speak in the tongues of mortals and of angels,
but do not have love,

I am a noisy gong or a clanging cymbal.
And if I have prophetic powers,
and understand all mysteries and all knowledge,
and if I have all faith, so as to remove mountains,
but do not have love, I am nothing.
If I give away all my possessions,
and if I hand over my body so that I may boast,
but do not have love, I gain nothing.

Love is patient; love is kind;
love is not envious or boastful or arrogant or rude.
It does not insist on its own way;
it is not irritable or resentful;
it does not rejoice in wrongdoing,
but rejoices in the truth.
It bears all things, believes all things,
hopes all things, endures all things.

Love never ends.
But as for prophecies, they will come to an end;
as for tongues, they will cease;
as for knowledge, it will come to an end.
For we know only in part,
and we prophesy only in part;
but when the complete comes,
the partial will come to an end.
When I was a child, I spoke like a child,
I thought like a child, I reasoned like a child;
when I became an adult,
I put an end to my childish ways.
For now we see in a mirror, dimly,
but then we will see face to face.
Now I know only in part; then I will know fully,
even as I have been fully known.
And now faith, hope, and love abide, these three;
And the greatest of these is love.

Brian Wren

What is love?

People stand in a circle holding hands. The leader breaks the circle and begins walking in a spiral pattern towards the middle of the circle. Everyone else continues holding hands and follows the leader. Eventually the leader will get to the middle of the circle and people will be in a tight spiral around the leader.

The leader then begins to unwind the spiral by walking outwards, again in a spiral pattern, and people follow on, still holding hands. When the spiral has unwound, people will discover that they are now standing in a circle facing outwards.

The significance of the movement is that in loving we reach deep within ourselves (the spiral going inwards), but our love is always channelled towards another person (so we end up facing outwards).

The starting position.

The inward spiral.

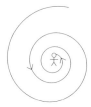

The middle point.

The outward spiral.

The finishing position.

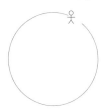

Lindsey Sanderson

Stories and Dramas

The giving tree

Once there was a tree . . . and she loved a little boy. Every day the boy would come and gather her leaves and make them into crowns and play king of the forest. He would climb her trunk and swing from her branches and eat her apples. They would play hide-and-seek and when he was tired, he would sleep in her shade.

The boy loved the tree . . . very much.

And the tree was happy.

But time went by. The boy grew older and the tree was often alone.

Then one day the boy came to the tree and the tree said, 'Come, boy, come and climb my trunk and swing from my branches and eat apples and play in my shade and be happy.' 'I am too big to climb and play', said the boy, 'I want to buy things and have fun. I want some money.' 'I'm sorry,' said the tree, 'but I have no money. I have only leaves and apples. Take my apples, boy, and sell them in the city. Then you will have money and you will be happy.'

So the boy climbed up the tree and gathered her apples and carried them away.

And the tree was happy.

The boy stayed away for a long time . . . and the tree was sad.

Then one day the boy came back and the tree shook with joy and said, 'Come, boy, climb my trunk and swing from my branches and be happy.' 'I am too busy to climb trees', said the boy. 'I want a house to keep me warm,' he said, 'I want a wife and I want children, and so I need a house. Can you give me a house?' 'I have no house,' said the tree. 'The forest is my house, but you may cut off my branches and build a house. Then you will be happy.'

So the boy cut off her branches and carried them away to build his house.

And the tree was happy.

The boy stayed away for a long time.

When he came back she could hardly speak, she was so happy.

'Come, boy,' she whispered, 'come and play.' 'I am too old and sad to play,' said the boy. 'I want a boat that will take me far away from here. Can you give me a boat?' 'Cut down my trunk and make a boat,' said the tree. 'Then sail away and be happy.'

So the boy cut down her trunk and made a boat and sailed away. And the tree was happy – but not really.

After a long time the boy came back again. 'I am sorry, boy,' said the tree. 'My apples are gone.' 'My teeth are too weak for apples,' said the boy. 'My branches are gone,' said the tree, 'you cannot swing on them.' 'I am too old to swing on branches,' said the boy.

'My trunk is gone,' said the tree, 'you cannot climb.' 'I am too tired to climb,' said the boy. 'I am sorry,' sighed the tree, 'I wish that I could give you something . . . but I have nothing left. I am just an old stump. I am sorry . . .'.

'I don't need very much now,' said the boy, 'just a quiet place to sit and rest. I am very tired.' 'Well,' said the tree, straightening herself up as much as she could, 'well, an old stump is good for sitting and resting. Come, boy, sit down. Sit down and rest.'

And the boy did.

And the tree was happy.

Shel Silverstein

Who is my neighbour?

A conversation between God and Mo, a mortal being with lots to learn. The names of the neighbours and the countries mentioned should be changed to be appropriate to your context.

Mo: *(To an invisible neighbour)* Look, Mr Smith, how many times do I need to say that I am sorry. The boys don't kick the ball into your garden on purpose, but the garden is the only safe place they can play nowadays. *(Pause.)* Yes, yes, I will speak to them again. *(Pause.)* And good day to you, Mr. Smith. *(Mo goes into the house and sits down.)* God! Why do we have to have neighbours?

God: Because you need them.

Mo: Who said that?

God: I did.

Mo: Who?

God: God . . . You did ask, you know.

Mo: Well, yes – but I didn't expect an answer.

God: Well, now we've started, we might as well continue.

Mo: Continue what? What do you mean? I only said something about my neighbour.

God: Exactly!!! You asked, 'Why do we have neighbours?' and I'm going to help you find the answer. But first you have to realise it's not just Mr Smith we are talking about.

Mo: Oh, yes, there's Mrs Jones too. She's always nice to the kids.

God: No, you have to look wider than that – it's not just the people who live on either side of you.

Mo: Of course, there's Mrs Brown at Number 2, and Mr and Mrs White at Number 5, and nice old Mr Black at Number 14 . . .

God: *(Interrupting)* When I said you had to look wider . . . I meant wide! *(said with feeling)*.

Mo: So you mean everyone in the street.

God: Y . . . e . . . s . . . but wider than that.

Mo: I've got it . . . you mean my family and friends. They're neighbours too in some ways.

God: Wider still.

Mo: Well, how about the people at work? They could be neighbours too . . . all except Mr Grimshaw – he's my boss.

God: We'll come back to Mr Grimshaw in a moment . . . but you must think even wider.

Mo: Well, I suppose I could think of all the people on my estate as my neighbours. It's an OK neighbourhood really, not like that place down the hill.

God: What's wrong with the people down the hill?

Mo: Well, you should know, God – they're a right bunch of no-hopers. Always getting into trouble for something or other. There's graffiti all over the place, they cause fights, half of them have been in prison at some point or other, and I wouldn't go near the place. It's so damp and dingy and they're so dirty – I might catch something.

God: Mo, have you got a Bible?

Mo: Yes . . . somewhere . . . Give me a minute and I'll find it. *(Rummages for the Bible.)* Ah . . . here it is.

God: Read Matthew 25 from verse 31. *(Mo fumbles through the Bible. He finds the passage and begins reading to himself. When he gets to verse 37 he reads verses 37–40 aloud.)*

Mo: So they are my neighbours too? *(incredulously).*

God: Yes, Mo, they're your neighbours too.

Mo: Next you'll be telling me that everyone in Scotland is my neighbour.

God: That's right.

Mo: But not the English – that's going too far!

God: Yes, Mo, even the English – and the Welsh and the Irish, for that matter, Mo. Everyone.

Mo: You mean everyone in the world! . . . That certainly is wide. But surely you're not serious – all these people are my neighbours?

God: Now we're getting somewhere . . . but there's more. As well as accepting that all people are your neighbours you have to love them.

Mo: Love all of them?

God: Yes, those you know, and those you don't know, and even the Smiths and Grimshaws of this world.

Mo: But why?

God: Mo, do you love me?

Mo: Well, yes, I am a Christian. I go to church every so often and I try to live a good life. I suppose I do love you – at least I try to, in my own small way.

God: Look around you, Mo. This world you live in, and the people in it came into being because of my love. I love this world. I even let my Son die for the sake of this world. Mo, if you love me you must love the world and everyone in it – you must love all your neighbours.

Mo: But how do you love someone far away, or worse still, someone you don't like?

God: To love someone doesn't mean that you always see eye to eye. It's about respecting and valuing people . . . Take your Bible again, Mo. Look up Micah chapter 6, verse 8 . . . *(Mo begins to thumb through the Bible.)* . . . Page 903, Mo.

Mo: *(Reads)* 'No, the Lord has told us what is good. What he requires of us is this: to do what is just, to show constant love, and to live in humble fellowship with our God.'

God: Think about it, Mo.

Lindsey Sanderson

Stories from Penrhys

In 1992 Penrhys, in South Wales, hosted an international youth-in-mission workcamp. For three weeks young people from Europe and beyond shared in the life of this community, taking part in running a holiday play scheme and building an open-air theatre. Built upon a ridge, overlooking the Rhondda valley, the Penrhys estate began life in the late 1960s. At the time of the camp around 3000 people lived on the estate, many of them unemployed. Around a third of the population then were under the age of 14 and many lived in single parent families. Social workers claimed that although Penrhys had 2 per cent of the Rhondda's population, it had 40 per cent of the Rhondda's social work case load.

The public image of Penrhys was often of a place that the 'rejects' of society were sent to when there was nowhere else to go. However, the experiences of the young people who took part in the workcamp belied that image. Yes, they did discover deep-rooted problems that would take years to solve, but they also found friendship, warmth and concern for the community that for many of them was lacking in their own communities. The following two stories describe some of the participants' experiences.

Margaret*

Imagine that you are standing on the steps of an open-air theatre, which you have just helped to build. A concert to celebrate its opening is in progress – a local band is singing Beatles' songs. In the crowd you notice a woman walking around with a tattered plastic bag asking for money. She is a known alcoholic and drug user. She comes up to you and holds out the bag – what do you do?

This was the scene that we were faced with at Penrhys. The responses of the youth-in-mission group were varied – some gave, most did not. Some of those who did not give had been advised not to by members of the church; others had felt unconvinced of her motives.

Once the woman had finished her collection she carried it up and presented it to the minister of the church in Penrhys. She embraced him and said, 'This is for the church.'

The minister was so moved by her gesture that he spoke about it in the next morning's service. How many of us felt bad about the way we treated Margaret, I can't say. However, I am sure that those of us who had refused to give Margaret money felt at the time that we were doing the right thing. How wrong we were shown to be. We had judged her incapable of a loving act.

(*not her real name)

In 1998 I had the opportunity to go back to Penrhys for a short time. While we were there the minister told us about how life in Penrhys had developed in the six years since the workcamp. The church now runs a number of Bible Study groups. Margaret had joined one of them.

The tree at Llanfair

In the garden next to the Penrhys church there are two trees. When we arrived, at the beginning of the workcamp, they were still reasonably young and although they had grown quite tall, they were still fragile. That they had survived as long as they had was a source of surprise and delight in a place where six-year-olds knew how to make and use petrol bombs. However, it was not to last.

One day during morning worship the minister told us that, as he had passed the two trees on the way to church, he had noticed that one of the trees had been split in half at the height of the strengthening post.

A feeling of sadness went through all of us as he recounted how the trees had been nurtured and cared for. Yet we all realized that, even though there had been two trees originally, one was still standing. I looked on it as a sign of the hope that was present in the community and in the church.

Tree surgeons came to look at the tree and wrote it off as beyond saving. However, the broken tree did not give up and towards the end of the workcamp it actually sprouted a leaf. Now that really was a sign of hope and life in Penrhys. As Job says:

For there is hope for a tree,
if it is cut down, that it will sprout again,
and that its shoots will not cease. (Job 14:7)

Lindsey Sanderson

Bearing one another's burden

Being situated in a deprived area in South Africa, our congregation had learnt from experience to obey Christ's command: 'You give them something to eat' (Matthew 14:16). So when it came to 'loving service' no stone was left unturned to make sure that the needs of the people in our community were met. Soup kitchens were launched; clothes, food, money, school fees, shelter and transport to hospitals were all provided. We were satisfied in the knowledge that the needs of the community had been addressed properly and in a Christ-like fashion.

Until on a particular Thursday morning, in the heart of winter, a man knocked on the pastor's door. The pastor opened the door confidently, knowing that whatever was needed, the church would be prepared to lend a hand.

The man at the door said, 'Pastor, I don't need clothes, all I need is your ear and your prayers. I am one of the many people who have AIDS. As a result I have lost everything I had in life: my job, my family, my home. My relatives have rejected me, because the clan to which I belong believes that a disease like this is a curse on them. For that reason I have had to leave. Pastor, I am not asking for shelter – I will find somewhere in the bushes – but I do need your prayers desperately.'

Now that was a new challenge for us. God chose that moment to call us to reach out to our brothers and sisters with AIDS, the people our society often rejects. The pastor invited the man to the weekly prayer service that evening. The usual format of the service was abandoned and the man was given an opportunity to tell his story to the congregation. Words of encouragement came from various people in the service and we all said prayers for him. Afterwards the man admitted that the service had made him feel like a 'somebody' again. And the best of all, it had made him realize that God still loved him and had sent his angels to protect him. The congregation later found the man a place in a shelter for people with AIDS. There he spent his last days under professional care and with loving support. He passed away a few months later.

But he left us a lasting legacy. He enabled us, as a congregation, to broaden our understanding of 'loving service'. Not only are we called to 'give them something to eat' but also, and perhaps more so, to 'bear one another's burden'.

Cathy Bott

Complete Liturgies

In Jesus' Footsteps

Guard your steps

Never be rash with your mouth, nor let your heart be quick to utter a word before God, for God is in heaven, and you upon earth; therefore let your words be few. (Ecclesiastes 5:2)

1. Greetings (in deaf-mute language)

JESUS: Show the palms of your hands. Point to the centre of your right hand and then do the same with your left hand, as if showing the marks of the cross on Jesus.

LIVES: Pass the fingers of both hands over the centre of your chest as if you are wiping something off your front.

IN ME: With both hands, point to the centre of your chest.

AND IN YOU: Opening your hands, offer them to another person.

2. Call to prayer

One: Guard your steps when you go to the house of God. Go near to listen rather than to offer the sacrifice of fools.

All: *Blessed is the one who comes in the name of the Lord! Hosanna in the highest!*

One: Peace be with you and your spirit!

All: *Peace be with you and your spirit!*

(Based on Ecclesiastes 5:1; Matthew 21:9)

3. Prayer

4. Song

Take off your sandals

1. Calling to confession (all are invited to take off their shoes)

One: Take off your sandals, for the place where you are standing
       is holy ground.
All: *Here we are, God, barefoot before you. Guide our feet into*
       the path of peace.

(Based on Exodus 3:5; Luke 1:79)

2. Silence

3. Prayer of confession

One: Therefore, because you trample on the poor, your feet are
       not worthy of the ground on which you stand.
All: *I feel my sin. I want to keep my feet away from every evil*
       path so that I might obey your word.

(Based on Amos 5:11; Psalms 119:101)

4. Guaicuru Kyrie (see p. 103)

5. Assurance of forgiveness (all are invited to put on shoes)

All: *It is God who arms me with strength and makes my way*
       safe. God makes my feet like the feet of a deer and enables
       me to stand on the heights.
One: Rise and go on your way; your faith has made you well!

(Psalms 18:32–33; Luke 17:19)

Wash my feet, oh God!

1. Litany of praise

One: Though the fig tree does not blossom and there are no
       grapes on the vines,
All: *Yet I will rejoice in the Lord, I will be joyful in God my*
       Saviour.
One: Though the olive crop fails and the fields produce no food,
All: *Yet I will rejoice in the Lord, I will be joyful in God my*
       Saviour.
One: Though there are no sheep in the pen and no cattle in the
       stalls,

All: *Yet I will rejoice in the Lord, I will be joyful in God my Saviour.*

(Based on Habakkuk 3:17–18)

2. Song of praise

3. Silent reading (based on the Gospel)

So he got up from the meal . . . took off his outer clothing . . . wrapped a towel around his waist . . . poured water into a basin and began to wash his disciples' feet, drying them with the towel that was wrapped around him.
'Lord, are you going to wash my feet?'
'You do not realize now what I am doing . . .'
'No, . . . you shall never wash my feet.'
'Unless I wash you, you have no share with me.'
'Do you understand what I have done for you?'
'So if I, your Lord and Teacher, have washed your feet, you also should wash one another's feet.'

(Based on John 13:1-20)

4. Song – The Washing of the Feet (see p. 95)

How beautiful are the feet

1. Intercessions

2. Dedication

One: How beautiful upon the mountains are the feet of the messenger who announces peace, who brings good news, who announces salvation, who says to Zion, 'Your God reigns.'

(Isaiah 52:7)

3. Song

4. Blessing

One: May the blessing of God
who creates and sustains life
who loves and struggles

be with you.
May God surround you
and challenge your
as you walk his Way.
In the name of the Father,
the Son and the Holy Spirit.

All: *Amen!*

Simei Monteiro

Part 4

Nurturing and Teaching

Hymns and Songs

We meet as friends at table

Words: Brian Wren
Music: Hal H. Hopson

MEAL OF LOVE
7.6.7.6.D.

We meet as friends at ta - ble, to lis - ten, and be heard, u - nit - ed by the Spir - it, at - ten - tive to the Word. Through

prayer and con - ver - sa - - tion we
tune our var - ied views to Christ, whose love has
made us the bear - ers of good news.

2. With food and drink for sharing
the table soon is spread.
The freedom meal of Jesus
is crowned with wine and bread,
and all, without exception,
may eat, and speak, and stay,
for this is Christ's own table
where none are turned away.

3. We share our lives and longings,
and when the meal is done
we pray as friends at table,
and promise to be one.
To Christ, and to each other,
we cheerfully belong:
apart, our hope is fruitless;
together, we are strong.

4. Fulfilled, and glad to follow
wherever Christ may lead,
we journey from the table
to love a world in need
with patience, truth and kindness,
that justice may increase
and all may sit at a table
in freedom, joy and peace.

Many yet one are the gifts of God's people

Words: Lindsey Sanderson
Legato, flowing

Music: Susan Heafield
Tune: SANDERSON

Many yet one are the gifts of God's people,
Talents and skills have been given for service,
Singing and baking, accounting and teaching,
People so varied, yet one in our purpose,

summoned and challenged to love and declare
sharing with others that God may be known,
friendship and comfort and mending the roof,
coming together as one family,

witness to God, who is love never ending,
gifts given freely and willingly offered,
visiting, preaching, empowering, or praying,
sharing the Gospel, enabling each other,

work for God's king-dom of jus-tice and peace.
blessed by the Spi-rit whose pre-sence is near.
such are the gifts which we of-fer to God.
this is our goal and the source of our hope.

Chorus

All who have faith ___ shall share in God's mis-sion,

tra-vel-ling peo-ple who dream and in - spire,

shar-ing our lives ___ with those we en - count-er,

of - fer - ing   hope,   as   we   jour - ney   with   God.

Remember

Noel Dexter

The land you love so dear - ly, now seems to fall a-

-part for spite and greed and ha - tred de - vour the mind and

heart. The sys-tem tram-ples on you, there is no hope, no

gain. In - jus-tice o - ver-whelms you, no com-fort, on - ly pain.

Chorus

Re - mem - ber ____ that we're stand-ing with you ____

Re - mem - ber ____ that you're not a - lone ____

____ To God we are pray-ing for you ____

And God _____ is still on the throne _____

2. You live each day in suff'ring,
   you cannot trust a friend.
   You strive for peace and justice,
   your trials have no end.
   Corruption in high places,
   deception night and day,
   'Where are you God?' you cry out,
   'Please hear me when I pray.'

3. We cannot join the frontline,
   yet we are in the fray.
   In faith we stand beside you,
   we're with you all the way.
   The battle is not ended;
   right always conquers wrong.
   Our God none can defeat and
   he makes the weak ones strong.

The church is like a table

Music: I-to Loh

Fred Kaan

The church is like a ta - ble, a

ta - ble that is round. It has no sides or

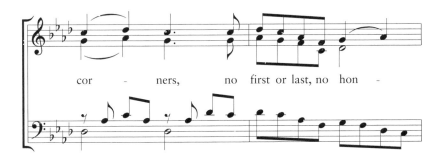

cor - ners, no first or last, no hon -

- ours; here peo - ple are in

one -ness and love to - geth - er bound.

2. The church is like a table
   set in an open house;
   no protocol for seating,
   a symbol of inviting,
   of sharing, drinking, eating;
   an end to 'them' and 'us'.

3. The church is like a table,
   a table for a feast
   to celebrate the healing
   of all excluded feeling
   (while Christ is serving, kneeling,
   a towel round his waist).

4. The church is like a table,
   where every head is crowned.
   As guests of God created,
   all are to each related;
   the whole world is awaited
   to make the circle round.

Tua Palavra é lâmpada

based on
Psalm 119:105

Words and music: Simei Monteiro

I know your word, your word is a lamp to my
Tu - a pa - la - vra é lâm - pa - da pa - ra - meus

feet, O God.
pés, O Deus.

I know your word is
Lâm-pa - da para-meus

light, O God;
pés e luz;

light for my path for -
luz para meu ca -

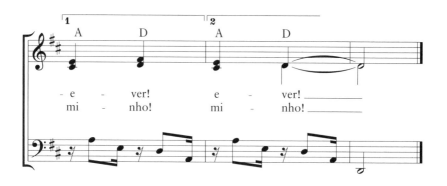

You are my body

Words: Brian Wren
Music: John Horman

WARNER
9.8.9.8.8.8.

1.'You are my bod-y!' Joy and won-der! As-sem-bled in our
2.'This is my bod-y!' Sim-ple Glo-ry! A cup of wine, a

Sav-iour's name, our scat-tered spir-its glad-ly gath-er the
loaf_ of bread feed us, and join us to the sto-ry of

Way of Je-sus to__ pro-claim. Come, Spi-rit, weave us
Christ, a-ris-en from the dead, whose Life, for-ev-er

into one, to show and tell what God has done.
flow - ing free, en - liv - ens all: O taste and see!

Harmony

3. At one in Christ, a - round the ta - ble where
4. We are your bod - y! One in Spir - it, dear

all may eat, and noth - ing pay, where all are
Christ, with all your church, we pray your bod - y

hon - oured and en - a - bled, and none are scorned or
lan - guage to in - her - it. Come, lead us in your

turned a - way,   we   pro - phe - sy, __ with   bro - ken
truth - ful   way!   To   seek __ for   what __ is   fair   and

bread,   a   world where ev - ery   child   is   fed.
right   shall   be __ our   du - ty   and   de - light!

Here's a new robe

Colossians 3:9–14

Words: Brian Wren

Music: Susan Heafield

Leader

All

C   C/E   F   C/E

Wear it to-mor-row, wear it to-day. ___ The

Amin7   Dmin7   C/G   G7   C

robe ___ of pa-tience, com-pas - sion and love.

Holy God, as you love us

Words: Brian Wren

Music: Susan Heafield

Ho - ly God, as you love us,

help us ___ to list - en ___ and love.

help us ___ to lis - ten and love.

Holy God, as you love us – 2

Words: Brian Wren   Music: Susan Heafield

Holy God, as you love us – 3

Words: Brian Wren

Music: Susan Heafield

Ho - ly God, as you love _____ us,

help us to lis - ten and love. _____

help us to lis - ten and love.

Swamin wahanse

Music: From Sri Lankan Liturgy
        transc. by: I-to Loh

Swa - min wa-han - se   Ka-ru-na _____ ka - l   ma - na-wa.
Lord, have mercy.

Chis-tus wa-han - se   Ka - ru - na ___   ka - l   ma - na - wa.
Christ, have mercy.

Calls to Worship

Fed by community:
the partnership of the global Church

L = Leader. R = Response.

L: From north and south and east and west
R: **Let all the people praise you, Lord;**
   let all the people praise you.
L: On the vast plains and in the deepest rainforest
R: **Let all the people praise you.**
L: In the mountains and land below sea level
R: **Let all the people praise you.**
L: In the driest deserts and wettest marsh
R: **Let all the people praise you.**
L: In city cathedrals and village churches
R: **Let all the people praise you.**
L: In a multitude of languages and an array of signs
R: **Let all the people praise you.**
L: In song and prayer, in drama and dance
R: **Let all the people praise you.**
L: In the sharing together of bread and wine
R: **Let all the people praise you, Lord;**
   let all the people praise you.

Lindsey Sanderson

Living in unity:
gathering God's people

Voice 1: A child
Voice 2: A young person/young adult
Voice 3: An adult/middle-aged person
Voice 4: An elderly person

1. God loves us all,
2. and so we come to worship God.
3. We come with eagerness and yet humility.
4. We come with our experiences of life's joy and pain.
2. We come seeking new ideas and directions for life.
3. We come in the busyness of living to nourish our spirit.
4. We come resting in the comfort and strength of God's presence.
1. God loves us all.

Lindsey Sanderson

People of the Covenant, draw near

One: People of the Covenant, draw near.
        Worship God, our Creator.

People: **We belong to the One who made us,
        whose love brought all things to birth.**

One: People of the Covenant, give thanks.
        In Christ, God makes a new covenant,
        with us, and all peoples.

People: **We praise God through Christ,
        who loves us, rescues us,
        and gives us new life.**

One: People of the Covenant, be strong!
        We are the body of Christ,
        a sign of God's living presence.

All: **May we live hopefully, and give hope to others;
        may we practise kindness, truthfulness and justice;
        may we live by faith, and be faithful.
        Thanks be to God!**

Brian Wren

Prayers

An invitation to the banquet

I invite you all,
who seek security
in land and possessions
to come and sit at the table
with those who have nothing to lose.

I invite you all,
who seek to be comfortable
in the circle of partner, family and friends
to come and sit at the table
with the different and strange.

I invite you all,
who seek power and status,
driven by ambition and insecurity,
to come and sit at the table
with the humble and gentle.

I invite you all,
who seek conformity
and live according to customs and codes
to come and sit at the table
with the free and the dancing.

I invite you all,
who seek stability,
accepting peace that is no peace,
to come and sit at the table
with the prophets and visionaries.

Christ, we want to accept your invitation,
empower us by your Spirit
to risk, to share, to venture, to dare,
to dream, to dance, to celebrate.
Make us worthy guests
at your great banquet of joy.

Francis Brienen

Living One, we belong to you

Living One, we belong to you,
for you have created all things.
Living Christ, we belong to you,
one body, showing your face to the world.
Living Spirit, by your power and presence,
we belong together, in Jesus Christ.

Brian Wren

May the Lover of Creation . . .

May the Lover of Creation, who gives birth to all things,
the Beloved, who meets us in Jesus,
and the Spirit who joins us in love,
Three-in-Communion, One God,
make us a community of hope and wholeness,
loving the last and the least,
making peace, resisting evil,
and caring for the good earth,
till all things are fulfilled
in the great dance of God;
and may God be praised,
now and for ever. Amen.

Brian Wren

Christ, our Teacher

Christ, our Teacher,
you open our minds to new possibilities,
and demand the best we can give.
Instruct us in the grammar of love,
that we may practise justice, compassion, and good faith,
and be shaped by your example,
inspired by your Spirit,
and in all things accountable to you,
our Wisdom, Word, and Way. Amen.

Brian Wren

An opening prayer

God of peace,
you hold the nations in your hand,
yet know and love us all.
By your Spirit, you gather us;
in Christ, you make us one;
As we come to Christ's table,
show us who we are,
what we can be,
and where we should go.
Set us free from all that is mean and wrong;
hold us in our pain and hurt;
and bring us from brokenness to wholeness,
through Jesus Christ, our Rescuer, Partner and Friend.
Amen.

Brian Wren

A prayer of confession

Voice A: People were bringing even infants to him that he might
touch them; and when the disciples saw it, they sternly
ordered them not to do it. But Jesus called for them and
said, 'Let the little children come to me, and do not stop

them; for it is to such as these that the kingdom of God belongs.' (Luke 18:15–16)

Voice B: Holy God, in the complexity of our living we fail to listen for the voices of children speaking words of simplicity and truth.
We presume they are empty jars waiting to be filled with our wisdom, insight and experience.
Give us grace to listen and learn together
as we journey in faith.

All: **Holy God, as you love us, help us to listen and love.**
Holy God, as you love us, help us to listen and love.
(spoken or sung; see pp. 155–7 for music)

Voice A: The Lord said to Samuel . . . 'I will send you to Jesse the Bethlehemite, for I have provided for myself a king among his sons.' Jesse made seven of his sons pass before Samuel, and Samuel said to Jesse, 'The Lord has not chosen any of these.' Samuel said to Jesse, 'Are all your sons here?' And he said, 'There remains yet the youngest, but he is keeping the sheep.' 'The Lord said, 'Rise and anoint him; for this is the one.' (1 Samuel 16:1b, 10, 11a, 12b)

Voice B: Holy God, too often we get so caught up
in the over-importance of our work and decision-making
that we fail to listen to the voices of young people
sharing new ideas and questioning convention.
We sideline their creativity
and channel their enthusiasm in our directions.
Give us grace to listen and learn together
as we journey in faith.

All: **Holy God, as you love us, help us to listen and love.**
Holy God, as you love us, help us to listen and love.

Voice A: There was also a prophet, Anna the daughter of Phanuel, of the tribe of Asher. She was of a great age, having lived with her husband seven years after her marriage, then as a widow to the age of eighty-four. She never left the temple but worshipped there with fasting and prayer night and

day. At that moment she came, and began to praise God
and to speak about the child to all who were looking for
the redemption of Jerusalem. (Luke 2:36–38)

Voice B: Holy God, amidst the speed of electronic communication
and the technology of our time
we fail to listen to the voices of the elderly amongst us.
We dismiss their experience as out-of-date
and become impatient when they speak the truth in
stories.
Give us grace to listen and learn together
as we journey in faith.

All: **Holy God, as you love us, help us to listen and love.**
Holy God, as you love us, help us to listen and love.

CWM

The road to Emmaus

Friend who walks our way,
   before the day is over
   change the focus of our seeing
   and help us to be aware of your presence.

Friend who walks our way,
   before the day is over
   capture our hearts and minds
   and help us to hear you
   in the voice of unexpected people.

Friend who walks our way,
   before the day is over
   show us the path to follow
   and help us to support those
   who have lost their way.

Friend who walks our way,
  before the day is over
  fill us with your love
  and may your reflection be seen in us
  as we break bread together.

Friend who walks our way,
  before the day is over,
  make yourself known to us
  and we will sing your praise
  and shout with many voices:
  Hallelujah, our God reigns.

                              Francis Brienen

Stories and Dramas

The story of the hand

Characters: Narrator, Thumb, Index Finger, Middle Finger, Ring Finger, Pinkie, Palm.
Props: A book and a table.

The sketch could simply be read using different voices, or it could be acted out more fully by the readers. If you are acting it out, it would be good to make a giant book so that people can see it, and to emphasize the point that each finger on its own can't lift the book.

Narrator: One day the five fingers of a hand had a big quarrel.

Thumb: I'm the most important! I'm the most important because I am different from the rest of you. I'm short and fat and I face a different direction to the rest of you.

Index Finger: Rubbish! I'm far more important than you. I am used to point at things, and to show people which way to go.

Middle Finger: You're both wrong. I am the biggest, so naturally I am the most important.

Ring Finger: None of you gets to wear beautiful rings like me. Diamonds, rubies, emeralds, gold and silver all adorn me. I am obviously the most important.

Pinkie: What about me? I may be the smallest, but remember that 'quality comes in small packages'. I think I am the most important.

Narrator: And so they continued arguing about who was the most important.

Middle: I'm the biggest.

Pinkie: Who says size matters?

Ring: Just look at my beautiful rings.

Index: But I do something useful when I point things out for people.

Thumb: There's only one of me, but four of you.

Narrator: Just then, Palm, who was by now completely fed up with their bickering, issued a challenge.

Palm: Whichever of you can pick up the book from the table is the most important one.

Narrator: Each finger in turn tried to pick up the book. First Thumb . . . then Index Finger . . . then Middle Finger . . . then Ring Finger . . . then Pinkie *(this could be mimed while the Narrator is speaking)*. But not a single one of them could pick up the book. Palm spoke again:

Palm: Right, it's clear. None of you are important. Now listen to me – I now want all five of you to make an effort to pick up the book. *(Together the fingers pick up the book.)*

Palm: See there, you managed to pick it up! Learn your lesson, fingers. No one is better than the others. We need each other, and that includes me. I can't do my job as a palm without you fingers to help me. We all need each other.

Lindsey Sanderson

The rainbow

The story can be read, or can be acted out with a narrator and the different colours and the rain being played by different people. If this is done it is good to dress people in their colour, or give them something of their colour to hold, perhaps a placard or a strip of fabric.

Another way the story can be used, particularly with younger children, is to give them a piece of coloured fabric and as the story is read, every time they hear their colour mentioned to wave their piece of fabric. The children can then be arranged into a rainbow at an appropriate point in the story.

Once upon a time all the colours in the world, red, green, blue, purple, orange, indigo, and yellow started to quarrel; each claimed that they were the best, the most important, the most useful, the favourite.

Green said, 'Clearly I am the most important.' 'Why?' said red. Green explained, 'I am the sign of life and hope. I was chosen for grass, trees and leaves – without me all the animals would die. Look out over the countryside and you will see green everywhere.'

Blue interrupted, 'You only think about the earth, but what about the sky and the sea? It is water that gives life and the clouds draw this up from the blue sea. The sky gives space and peace and serenity. Without my peace you would all be nothing but busybodies.'

Yellow chuckled, 'You are all so serious. I bring laughter, fun and warmth to the world. The sun is yellow. Every time you look at a sunflower, the whole world starts to smile. Without me there would be no fun.'

Orange started to blow its own trumpet next, 'I'm the most important, I'm the most important,' it said in a sing-song way. 'Oh no, you're not,' shouted purple and indigo who had been very quiet up to this point. Orange said, 'I am the colour of health and strength. I may be scarce but I am precious for serving the inner needs of human life. I carry all the most important vitamins. Think of carrots and pumpkins, oranges, mangoes and pawpaws. I don't hang around all the time, but when I fill the sky at sunrise or sunset, my beauty is so striking that no one gives another thought to any of you.'

Red could stand it no longer. It was very angry and shouted out, 'I'm the ruler of you all: blood, life's blood. I am the colour of danger and bravery. I am willing to fight for a cause. I bring fire in the blood. Without me the earth would be as empty as the moon. I am the colour of passion and of love; the red rose, poinsettia and poppy.'

Purple rose to its full height. It was very tall and spoke with great pomp, 'I am the colour of royalty and power. Kings, chiefs and bishops have always chosen me, for I am a sign of authority and wisdom. People do not question me, they listen and obey.'

Indigo spoke much more quietly than all the others, but just as determinedly, 'Think of me. I am the colour of silence. You hardly notice me, but without me, you all become superficial. I represent thought and reflection, twilight and deep waters. You need me for balance and contrast, for prayer and for inner peace.'

And so the colours went on boasting, each convinced that they were the best. Red is best; no, green is best; no, indigo is best. Purple is more important; no, orange is more important; yellow is best; blue is best of all.

Their quarrelling became louder and louder. Suddenly, there was a startling flash of brilliant white lightning; thunder rolled and boomed. Rain started to pour down relentlessly. The colours all crouched down in fear, drawing close to one another for comfort. (*Encourage colours to crouch down together as if scared.*)

Then rain spoke, 'You foolish colours, fighting among yourselves, each trying to dominate the rest. Do you not know that God made you all, each for a special purpose, unique and different? He loves you all. He wants you all. Join hands with one another and come with me. We will stretch you across the sky in a great bow of colour, as a reminder that God loves you all, that you can live together in peace; a promise that God is with you – a sign of hope for tomorrow. Now let's get you organized, red is first, then orange, then yellow, now green, now blue, indigo and purple.' *(Get colours to stand in line holding hands in order of a rainbow.)*

And so whenever God has used a good rain to wash the world, he puts the rainbow in the sky. When we see it we should remember that God wants us all to love and value each other as part of God's family, just as red, orange, yellow, green, blue, indigo and purple are part of the family of colours.

Indian legend adapted by Lindsey Sanderson

Complete Liturgies

We all belong to Christ's body

An order of worship based on 1 Corinthians 12.

We all belong to Christ's body

Responsive reading: 1 Corinthians 12:12–17

Leader: For just as the body is one and has many members,

Group A: and all the members of the body, though many, are one body,

All: **so it is with Christ.**

Group B: For in the one Spirit we were all baptized into one body –

Group C: Jews or Greeks, slaves or free –

All: **and we were all made to drink of one Spirit.**

Leader: Indeed, the body does not consist of one member but of many.

Group A: If the foot would say, 'Because I am not a hand, I do not belong to the body,'

Group B: that would not make it any less a part of the body.

Group C: And if the ear would say, 'Because I am not an eye, I do not belong to the body,'

Group B: that would not make it any less a part of the body.

All: **If the whole body were an eye, where would the hearing be?**
If the whole body were hearing, where would the sense of smell be?

Song: 'If one member suffers' (page 172)

Based on 1 Corinthians 12:26

If one member suffers

4-part Canon

I Cor. 12:26

Music: I-to Loh

If one— mem-ber suf-fers, all suf - fer to - ge-ther. If
Na chit-thé — siú - kho, — pah - thé tâng siú - khó. — Chit -

one part is praised, all oth - ers share its joy.
- thé siú êng - kng, pah - thé — tâng khòai-lok.

We all need one another

Responsive reading: 1 Corinthians 12:18–26

Leader: But as it is, God arranged the members in the body, each one of them, as he chose.

All: **If all were a single member, where would the body be?**

Group A: As it is, there are many members, yet one body.

Group B: The eye cannot say to the hand, 'I have no need of you,'

Group C: nor again the head to the feet, 'I have no need of you.'

Leader: On the contrary, the members of the body that seem to be weaker are indispensable,

Group A: and those members of the body that we think less honourable we clothe with greater honour,

Group B: and our less respectable members are treated with greater respect;

Group C: whereas our more respectable members do not need this.

Group A: But God has so arranged the body, giving the greater honour to the inferior member,

Group B: that there may be no dissension within the body,

Group C: but the members may have the same care for one another.

All: **If one member suffers, all suffer together with it; if one member is honoured, all rejoice together with it.**

Song: 'If one member suffers'

We share others' sufferings and honours

Responsive reading: 1 Corinthians 12:26–27

Group A: If one member suffers, all suffer together with it;

Group B: if one member is honoured, all rejoice together with it.

All: **Now you are the body of Christ and individually members of it.**

Meditation: Sharing others' sufferings and honours

Song: 'If we love one another' (go to page 99)

I John 4:12   Music: I-to Loh

Prayers of intercession

Response: *'Swamin wahanse'* (go to page 158)

Music: From Sri Lankan Liturgy
      transc. by: I-to Loh

We commit ourselves for love and justice

Song: 'The Lord has told us what is good' (go to page 41)

Words: Micah 6:8
Music: I-to Loh

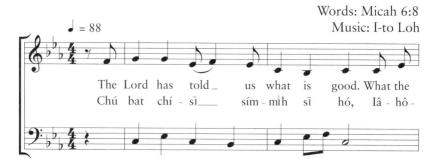

The Lord has told _ us what is good. What the
Chú bat chí - sī___ sím - mi̍h sī hó, Iâ - hô-

Karen benediction

From the Karen people of Myanmar.

Mar ba zey _____ chañ mar ba
May the Lord _____ bless you with
May the Lord _____ be al - ways

zey, Pañ lo hmwe ye lo ey ga,
joy, like the flow - ers with their scent,
near, lead you, keep you from all ill,

Htaw–a–ziñ shwiñ lañ ja ba zey, Ey, __ ey jañ bo ley,__
like the swirl on flow-ing stream. Yes,__ yes, go for - ward,_
sow in you the thirst for peace. Yes,_ peace with jus - tice__

___ Bey ba ya Kiñ kwa zey bo ley.
___ and let the LORD be at your side.
___ to con - quer dark - ness by God's Light.

I-to Loh

A communion meditation:
offering the gifts of bread and wine

The gifts of bread and wine are brought to the table, together with a bowl of flour, a jug of water, a small bottle of oil, a small bowl of yeast, some salt and a bunch of grapes. They are brought by a man, woman and two children who lead the meditation on the gifts of bread and wine. The responses are by the congregation as a whole. This meditation can be used in preparation for communion.

Child 1:   We have brought the gifts of bread and wine to share at the feast with Jesus.

Man: Let us remind ourselves of what the bread and wine mean.

Woman: If we left the flour on its own in the bowl it would be wasted. We must add water to the flour. As the bread and water mix together they turn into dough; the water and the flour become one.
(while the words are spoken, the water is poured into the bowl with the flour)

Man: As the flour and water become one, so we are united by the water of our baptism.

People: The water of our baptism unites us.

Woman: We add oil to the dough to make it soft and flexible.
(the oil is added to the dough)

Man: The oil reminds us of our anointing by the Holy Spirit.

Child 1:   The Holy Spirit gives us grace to be open to others.

Child 2:   The Holy Spirit gives us grace to care for their needs.

People: The Holy Spirit anoints us.

Child 2:   We add the salt next.
(the salt is added to the dough)

Woman: A little salt will improve the flavour of the bread.

Child 1:   Jesus says we are the salt of the earth.

Man: We are to bring flavour and life to a world which is bland and tasteless.

People: Jesus calls us 'the salt of the earth'.

Man: For our bread to be complete we need to add yeast to the dough.
(the yeast is added)

Child 1:   This will make the bread rise and good to eat.

Child 2:   Jesus also spoke about yeast.

Woman:	He said that the kingdom of God is like yeast that a woman took and mixed with flour.
People:	**The vision of God's kingdom inspires us.**
Man:	Lastly, we must bake the bread in the oven.
Child 2:	When it is ready, we will break it and share it.
Child 1:	Jesus calls us to share what we have with people in need.
Woman:	He said: 'Just as you did it to one of the least of these, you did it to me.'
People:	**Our sharing transforms life.**
Child 2:	We have made the bread, what about the wine?
Man:	The wine is made with grapes that have come from the vineyard.
Woman:	Jesus said, 'I am the vine and you are the branches.'
Child 1:	With other people of faith, we are the branches.
People:	**We are united in Jesus as the branches are united to the trunk of the tree.**
Child 2:	The grapes grow together in a bunch.
Child 1:	So we need to grow together as a community.
Woman:	A community of people who share together.
Man:	A community of people who care for one another.
People:	**We are a community bound together in love.**
Man:	For the grapes to become wine, these beautiful fruits must be crushed.
Woman:	The crushing of the grapes reminds us that Jesus was also crushed in death.
Child 1:	Yet he rose again to bring us new life.
Child 2:	Life in all its fulness.
People:	**In Christ Jesus we have new life.**
Woman:	Once the grapes have been crushed we must wait.
Child 1:	We must wait until the time is right to drink the wine.
Man:	We are waiting for the right time.
Child 2:	The right time when God's reign will come.
People:	**We are people of hope and promise.**
Child 1:	We bring gifts of bread and wine to share in Jesus' great Feast.
Child 2:	This is what they mean for us.
People:	**Let us celebrate the Feast.**

Simei Monteiro and Lindsey Sanderson

Part 5

Caring for Creation

Hymns and Songs

The God of us all

From Psalm 91 & Ephesians 5: 1–2

SANTA MESA

Words: Ron O'Grady
Music: I-to loh

The God of us all is our Fa - ther, he

guides us when we are in dan - ger, he

calls us to hon - our the stran - ger.

Great is the LORD, ev - er a - dored!

May be accompanied by a zither or guitar.

The God of us all is our Mother,
she teaches us her truth and beauty,
she shows us a love beyond duty.
Great is the LORD, ever adored!

Our God is a Father and Mother,
surrounding us all with protection,
to give to the world new direction.
Great is the LORD, ever adored!

Thank you, God, for water, soil and air

This hymn can also be used as a congregational reading, with one side of the congregation (A) saying the 'thanksgiving' part of each stanza, the other side (B) saying the confession part, and with everyone joining in the last line and the whole of the final stanza (All). When sung as a hymn, ignore these directions.

Words: Brian Wren
Music: John Weaver

AMSTEIN
9.10.10.9.

-new _____ the face _____ of the earth.

A: Thank you, God, for minerals and ores,
    the basis of all building, wealth and speed.
B: Forgive our reckless plundering and waste.
All: **Help us renew the face of the earth.**

A: Thank you, God, for priceless energy,
    stored in each atom, gathered from the sun.
B: Forgive our greed and carelessness of power.
All: **Help us renew the face of the earth.**

A: Thank you, God, for weaving nature's life
    into a seamless robe, a fragile whole.
B: Forgive our haste, that tampers unaware.
All: **Help us renew the face of the earth.**

A: Thank you, God, for making planet earth
    a home for us, and ages yet unborn.
B: Help us to share, consider, save and store.
All: **Come and renew the face of the earth.**

Send out your Spirit

Words: Brian Wren
Music: Simei Monteiro

Send out your spirit, ___ send out; re-

new the sea and the land. With

lov - ing care for the earth, we'll

sing your prais - es   for - e - ver! _____

* Can be used as an Introduction or just the 'Ostinato'.
  The 'Ostinato' accompaniment can also be sung by a choir (humming).

God's glory (praise)

One of three responses to go with Wesley Ariarajah's 'A Litany on creation'.

Words: Brian Wren   Music: Susan Heafield

-lu — — ia, al - le - lu — — ia!

Earth is abused (repentance)

One of three responses to go with Wesley Ariarajah's 'A Litany on creation'.

Words: Brian Wren   Music: Susan Heafield

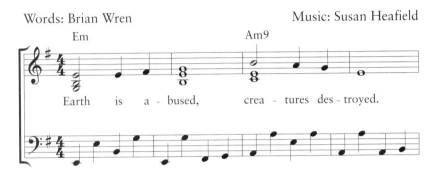

Earth is a - bused, crea - tures des - troyed.

Greed goes with pride, griev - ing God weeps.

rit .....

Let us weep with God, pray - ing to find

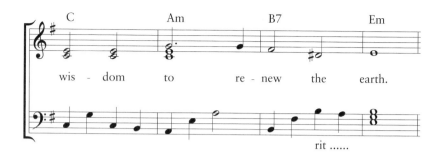

wis - dom   to   re - new   the   earth.

rit ......

Can we believe . . . (thanksgiving)

One of three responses to go with Wesley Ariarajah's 'A Litany on creation'.

Words: Brian Wren   Music: Susan Heafield

sign._____ All shall be well. O_____

thanks be to God._____

Responses

Three responses to go with Wesley Ariarajah's 'A Litany on creation'.

Noel Dexter

We praise you, O God: And we glo - ri-fy your name.

O, for-give us, dear Lord, And grant_ us your peace.

We praise you, we thank you for your good-ness to _ us all.

189

Loving God, forgive

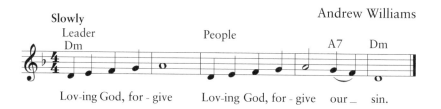

Slowly   Andrew Williams

Lov-ing God, for - give   Lov-ing God, for - give   our _   sin.

Calls to Worship

The earth belongs to God

From Psalm 24:1.

L = Leader. R = Response.

L: The earth belongs to God.
R: **The earth belongs to God.**
L: We, humankind,
    hold the planet in our hands.
R: **The earth belongs to God.**

L: The land belongs to God.
R: **The land belongs to God.**
L: Land is God's gift,
    yielding food enough for all.
R: **The land belongs to God.**

L: The world belongs to God.
R: **The world belongs to God.**
L: All living things
    are entrusted to our care.
R: **The world belongs to God.**

Brian Wren

Our Creator calls us

L = Leader. R = Response.

L: Our Creator calls us,
    Our Maker gathers us,
R: **Let us come into God's presence with thanksgiving.**

191

L: In wisdom God gave birth to all things,
loving and cherishing the earth.
R: Let us love God's earth
  and rejoice in its abundant life.

L: In Christ, God loves us to the uttermost.
R: Let us become what we are, the body of Christ,
  walking together in justice and peace.

Brian Wren

In the beginning God said . . .

One: In the beginning God said, 'Let there be light.'
All: And there was light and it was good.
One: Then God said, 'Let there be land in the middle of the seas.'
All: And there was land and it was good.
One: And God said, 'Let there be animals – all sorts of animals.'
All: And they were good.
One: Then God said, 'Let there be people made in our image.'
All: And we, too, are part of God's creation.

Cathy Bott

Prayers

A prayer of confession

Living God,
we praise you for the beauty of creation,
we praise you for the rich variety of life,
we praise you for your delight in us, your people,
we praise you for giving us the care for all that lives.
We praise you for your trust in us.

Loving God,
forgive us our indifference,
our cruelty and our lack of care.
Fill us with your love
so that even yet we may fulfil your purpose for us,
turning everything that lives and breathes and grows
to goodness.
Through Jesus Christ, our Lord,
Amen.

Cathy Bott

A prayer of commitment

One: God has given us the world to care for;
let us commit ourselves to caring for God's creation.
All: **Amen. We respond to God's gift.**

One: Let us use our control over the natural world wisely and
sensitively.
All: **Amen. We dedicate our efforts to serving God's Kingdom.**

One: Let us exercise our husbandry of animals and birds without
exploitation.

All: Amen. May no creature suffer cruelty at our hands.

One: Let us nurture green and growing things for nourishment and beauty.
All: Amen. May we use all advances in knowledge to enrich life on earth.

One: Let us do all we can to keep pure the soil, the air and the water that give us life.
All: Amen. May we cherish the earth.

One: Let us resist the temptation to exploit and pollute for profit and convenience.
All: Amen. We cannot serve God and money.

One: Let us love our neighbours and open our hearts to the needs of the poor.
All: Amen. Jesus said: 'There is more happiness in giving than in receiving.'

One: Let us pass on to our children and the generations yet to come a world fit to be called home for the whole created order.
All: Amen. May we learn to appreciate the wonder of God's world.

All: In the name of Jesus Christ,
Amen.

Cathy Bott

Bright and beautiful God

Bright and beautiful God,
thank you for our world,
a place full of beauty and variety.
Thank you for the winds and the waves,
the stars in the sky,
the changing of the seasons,
the animals in all their splendour.
Thank you, God, for this beautiful gift.

Thank you, God, for the gift of people,
men, women and children,
of many colours and creeds,
in different shapes and sizes,
with many gifts and talents,
all made and loved by you.
Thank you, God, for this beautiful gift.

Thank you, God, for the variety of life.
Everything points to your love and glory.

Francis Brienen

Litanies

A litany on creation

Voice: The earth is the Lord's and all that is in it, the world, and those who live in it. *(Psalm 24:1)*

Leader: The heavens are telling the glory of God, and the firmament proclaims his handiwork. Day to day pours forth speech, and night to night declares knowledge. *(Psalm 19:1–2)*

People: God's glory fills creation, all living things, all of the earth. God is good! Sing and be glad. Alleluia, Alleluia!
(Sung response, see p. 183. Alternatively, the first response on p. 189 may be used.)

Voice: O Lord, how manifold are your works! In wisdom you have made them all; the earth is full of your creatures. *(Psalm 104:24)*

Leader: These all look to you to give them their food in due season; when you give to them, they gather it up; when you open your hand, they are filled with good things. When you hide your face, they are dismayed; when you take away their breath, they die and return to their dust. When you send forth your spirit, they are created and you renew the face of the ground. *(Psalm 104:27–30)*

People: God's glory fills creation, all living things, all of the earth. God is good! Sing and be glad. Alleluia, Alleluia!
(Sung response.)

Voice: Hear the word of the Lord, O people of Israel; for the Lord has an indictment against the inhabitants of the land. *(Hosea 4:1)*

Leader: There is no faithfulness or loyalty, and no knowledge of God in the land. Swearing, lying and murder, and stealing and adultery break out; bloodshed follows bloodshed. Therefore the land mourns, and all who live in it languish; together with the wild animals and the birds of the air, even the fish of the sea are perishing. *(Hosea 4:1–3)*

People: **Earth is abused, creatures destroyed. Greed goes with pride, grieving God weeps. Let us weep with God, praying to find wisdom to renew the earth.**
(Sung response, see p. 185. Alternatively, the second response on p. 189 may be used.)

Voice: With what shall I come before the Lord, and bow myself before God on high? *(Micah 6:6)*

Leader: He has told you, O mortal, what is good; and what does the Lord require of you, but to do justice, and to love kindness, and to walk humbly with your God? *(Micah 6:8)*

People: **Earth is abused, creatures destroyed. Greed goes with pride, grieving God weeps. Let us weep with God, praying to find wisdom to renew the earth.**
(Sung response.)

Voice : I consider that the sufferings of this present time are not worth comparing with the glory about to be revealed to us. *(Romans 8:18)*

Leader: For the creation waits with eager longing for the revealing of the children of God . . . the creation itself will be set free from its bondage to decay and will obtain the freedom of the glory of the children of God. *(Romans 8:19–21)*

People: **God's glory fills creation, all living things, all of the earth. God is good! Sing and be glad. Alleluia, Alleluia!**
(Sung response, see p. 183. Alternatively, the first response on p. 189 may be used.)

Voice: Then I saw a new heaven and a new earth; for the first heaven and the first earth had passed away, and the sea was no more. *(Revelation 21:1–2)*

Leader: And the one who was seated on the throne said, 'See, I am making all things new' . . . Then the angel showed me the river of the water of life, bright as crystal, flowing from the throne of God and of the lamb . . . On either side of the river is the tree of life with its twelve kinds of fruit, producing its fruit each month; and the leaves of the tree are for the healing of the nations. Nothing accursed will be found there any more. *(Revelation 21:5; 22:1–3)*

People: **Can we believe that all shall be well, that earth shall be fair, creation renewed? Yes, we believe! Christ is our sign. All shall be well. Thanks be to God.**
(Sung response, see p. 187. Alternatively, the third response on p. 189 may be used.)

Eternal God,
Before the wind swept over the face of the waters,
you were.
Before the first ray of light pierced the darkness of the void,
you were.
Before the power of your word brought meaning into chaos,
you were.
(Silence.)
It is in you that we live, and move and have our being.
Out of the dust of the earth you fashioned us
and called us to care for the earth.
Teach us to enjoy the beauty of creation.
Help us to discern your presence in it,
and enable us to respect all life.

Living God,
Like a tree planted by the rivers of water,
our lives have been nourished by your faithfulness and love.
Kindle the fire of love in our hearts
that we may love you and all that you have made.

Wesley Ariarajah

Symbolic Acts

Modelling

Each person is given a small amount of plasticine or modelling clay and invited to model something from God's creation. They could, for example, make a tree or an animal. The models are kept before them as everyone joins in a celebration of the 'goodness' of creation, in song and prayer.

After celebrating the goodness of creation, people are reminded of humanity's destruction and exploitation of nature. To symbolize this they are asked to destroy their models. They then join in an act of confession.

After the act of confession all are given the opportunity to recommit themselves to the care of creation and to promise to take concrete action as an outward sign of this commitment. They are then invited to take their modelling clay and to model a symbol of their proposed action. For example, they could model a tree as a symbol for planting a tree or supporting an organization which protects the rain forest. They could model food as a symbol of buying organic food or supporting fair trading.

Lindsey Sanderson

Stories and Dramas

Miss World visits the doctor

There are two characters, Miss World (or Mother Earth, if you prefer) and a Doctor. Miss World needs to be wearing a map of the earth, so she can explain her symptoms. This could be done as a sandwich board with the globe represented on both sides. The Doctor needs a white coat and a stethoscope, or other symbols of a doctor.

The specific references (in italics) to particular world events may need to be changed, depending on your context and on what is happening in the world at the time when the sketch is performed.

Dr = Doctor. M W = Miss World.

Dr: Hello, Miss World. You look in a bad way. What seems to be the problem?

M W: Well, I just feel ill all over. I'm not sure where to start.

Dr: Well, my dear, what are the symptoms?

M W: Well, firstly there's my head. I feel as if I'm overheating up here in the arctic. *(Taps head.)* Beads of perspiration keep running down my forehead and off the end of my nose! It makes the rest of my body feel all peculiar – it's as if my temperature keeps changing all the time. I feel that I am getting hotter and hotter. I feel out of sorts.

Dr: *(Makes reassuring noises.)*

M W: And then there's this dryness. It's not quite in my throat but it's close enough. It's here . . . in Africa. *(Points to Africa.)* I'm always thirsty, but even when I have a drink it doesn't seem to help. There also seem to be great clouds of dust around which just make things worse. *(Pause.)*

And around here, and here, and here *(pointing to areas of the world where the forests are being destroyed)* it's horrible! I've got all these bald patches – it's like my hair falling out, my skin peeling off and having ulcers all rolled into one. I know it's just that all these trees are being cut down, but I'm really feeling bare in the Amazon, in Indonesia and up here in Canada and Scandinavia too.

Mind you, I have more problems in Canada and Scandinavia. Yes, I cough and splutter all the time. It's the pollution and acid rain – horrible stuff to breathe in. It really gets to the back of your throat. Sometimes it can be really hard to find clean air.

That's not the only problem I have with pollution, though. Around this part of the world *(points to Western Europe and North America)* I get these awful stabbing pains. They are especially sore when they dump more rubbish into holes in the ground or pour tankfuls of chemical soup into the North Sea. *(Pause.)*

Of course, these stabbing pains are different from the shooting pains I get round Bosnia, Ireland, Israel/Palestine and many other places – they really are sore. *(Pause.)*

I think those are all my aches and pains . . . but I did want to ask you about those tests you did, Doctor . . . My bottom feels like a pin cushion!

Dr: Oh yes . . . the nuclear tests . . . perhaps we shouldn't have done those!

MW: Do you mean they were unnecessary? Oh my poor Pacific Islands! They will never be the same.

Dr: Oh you poor old thing, Miss World! You really have been having a dreadful time, haven't you? I'm afraid this all sounds like a very bad case of The Humans.

MW: Humans? . . . You mean human beings? Is this disease curable? What can be done about it, Doctor?

Dr: Well, a lot can be done . . . but quite frankly, it depends on the humans themselves. These shooting pains in Bosnia and Ireland and Israel/Palestine – they'll all have to stop fighting and try some TLC *(Tender Loving Care)*, not TCP *(a liquid antiseptic)*. And then those symptoms affecting you up top – there's a hole in your ozone layer. I know they've stopped using CFCs but it's really not enough – more work needed there. Global warming is causing a lot of your problems, and making you feel utterly miserable . . .

That dryness you spoke about, where was that?

MW: In Africa.

Dr: Hmmmm . . . We'll have to promote rainfall somehow . . . You must stop them cutting down trees and preserve the water you do have. If we did a little operation to replant round this area *(points to Africa)* and this area *(points to Indonesia)* and if we have sustainable forests up here *(points to Scandinavia)*, it would go a long way towards stopping all the deforestation you're experiencing . . . It's a horrible feeling when your hair and skin start to go . . . I do sympathize.

Now was there some other problem?

MW: Yes, the coughing and spluttering – and the stabbing pain up here *(points to northern Europe)*.

Dr: Definitely pollution! Why don't you get the humans to pick up litter, and recycle as much as they can? And how about campaigning for more use of wind power and water power instead of burning fossil fuels and creating all that acid and smoke? Poor Miss World! No wonder you can hardly breathe.

MW: Right . . . and does this mean I won't have to have any more of those nasty nuclear tests, Doctor?

Dr: Well . . . if the humans can just try some of the remedies I've mentioned and can begin to see that they all need to help each other – and you, Miss World – we'll not require those tests. The very best treatment is a real change in lifestyle and a lot of Tender Loving Care.

MW: Well, thank you, Doctor – there does seem to be some hope, if only I can get those humans to listen and start looking after me. Tender Loving Care – it shouldn't be too difficult.

Lindsey Sanderson

Greyfriars Bobby

Bobby was a Skye terrier who belonged to Auld Jock Gray who lived in Edinburgh, Scotland, in the nineteenth century. According to local folklore, Bobby and Jock were inseparable. They spent their days together in the Grassmarket where Jock worked, and each day they went to a local tavern. Jock had a meal there and Bobby had a bun and a bone.

Auld Jock died in 1858 and was buried in the nearby Greyfriars' Churchyard. Just as they had been inseparable in life, so Bobby and Jock were inseparable after Jock's death. Bobby lived for another fourteen years and spent them living by his master's grave. He was cared for by the local people and when he too died in 1872, Bobby was buried close to Auld Jock.

Bobby's statue just outside Greyfriars' Church is a popular tourist attraction in Edinburgh, and reminds us of the faithfulness of love, not only between a man and his dog but also of the love which God has for creation.

Lindsey Sanderson

Acknowledgements

PART 1: PROCLAIMING THE GOOD NEWS

Hymns and Songs

'To Christ our hearts now given'. Words: Brian Wren © 1996 Hope Publishing Co., Carol Stream, IL 60188, USA. Music: Johann Steurlein, 'Wie Lieblich Ist Der Maien' (1575). © 1995 Stainer & Bell Ltd for the World except USA, Canada, Australia and New Zealand. Reprinted by permission.

'I'll sing my faith'. Words © Noel Dexter; music © 1999 Praise Partners Publishing. All rights reserved.

'The time has come'. Words: based on Mark 1:15. Music: © I-to Loh.

'O what a glorious day!' Words and music: © Noel Dexter.

'Enter into God's house'. Words and music: © Noel Dexter.

'O worship the Lord'. Music © Noel Dexter; words: J. S. B. Monsell, 1811–75 (adapted).

Calls to Worship

'Come and receive'. Words: Brian Wren. Music: Susan Heafield. © 1999 Praise Partners Publishing. All rights reserved.

'God said, "Let there be light"'. © Brian Wren.

'We are ambassadors for Christ'. © Brian Wren.

'Follow the King of kings'. © Arao Litsure.

'Christ is the world's true light'. © Brian Wren.

Invocations

'Christ among us'. © Brian Wren.

'We do not proclaim ourselves'. © Brian Wren.

Prayers

'A cloud of witnesses'. © Francis Brienen.

'Prayers for women and men on their journeys'. © Lindsey Sanderson.

'We are the body of Christ'. © Brian Wren.

'Assurance of God's grace'. © Brian Wren.
'God of love, faithful and gracious forever'. © Brian Wren.
'Holy God, hear our cry'. © Brian Wren.
'Dear friends, we are created . . .' © Brian Wren.
'God of all nations'. © Brian Wren.
'Here is good news'. © Brian Wren.
'Let us confess our sin'. © Brian Wren.
'Trinitarian praise and adoration'. © Brian Wren.
'Here I am, send me'. © Lindsey Sanderson.

Litanies

'A litany of faith and hope'. © S. Wesley Ariarajah.
'Celebrating the promises'. © S. Wesley Ariarajah.

Symbolic Acts

'Gifts for life'. © Lindsey Sanderson.
'Unbinding fear's knots'. Adapted from *Joy is our Banquet: Resources for Everyday Worship* by K. Wehlander, © 1996 The United Church of Canada Publishing House.

Stories and Dramas

'A better way'. © Revd Steven M. Notis, Cape Elizabeth United Methodist Church, Cape Elizabeth, Maine, USA.

Blessings

'Peace and love'. © Noel Dexter.
'Parent of Light, Holy and Good'. © Brian Wren.
'As we go in Christ'. © Brian Wren.
'Let us go in peace'. © Brian Wren.

PART 2: TRANSFORMING SOCIETY

Hymns and Songs

'The Lord has told us what is good'. Words: based on Micah 6:8. Music: © 1995 I-to Loh.
'This we can do for justice'. Words: © 1975; 1995 Stainer & Bell Ltd for the World except USA, Canada, Australia and New Zealand. Reprinted by permission. Music © I-to Loh.
'Building a just society'. © Christian Conference of Asia.
'From this time onwards'. Words: a Bunun hymn from Taiwan, translated by I-to Loh and James Minchin. © I-to Loh and James Minchin. Music: 'U-i-hi', a Bunun melody from Taiwan.

'One family'. Words and music: © Noel Dexter.
'Let justice be our guide'. Words: © Brian Wren & Arao Litsure. Music: © Arao Litsure.
'Eh Vukani (Hey, people of God)'. Words & music: © Arao Litsure.
'To break the chains'. Words: © S. Wesley Ariarajah & Brian Wren. Music: © I-to Loh 1998, adapted from the Kachin melody 'Myanmar'.
'Lead us in paths of truth'. Words: © Brian Wren. Music: © 1998 I-to Loh.
'Living in a world that suffers'. Words: extracted from Brian Wren's hymn, 'Speechless in a world that suffers', © 1995 Stainer & Bell Ltd for the World except USA, Canada, Australia and New Zealand. Reprinted by permission. Music: © 1998 I-to Loh.

Calls to Worship

'Listen and look'. © Brian Wren.
'For national occasions'. © Brian Wren.

Prayers

'Gifts'. © Francis Brienen.
'A prayer for Passiontide'. © Francis Brienen.
'Treading down the evils'. © Francis Brienen.
'Confession'. © Andrew Williams.
'A guiding star'. © Francis Brienen.
'An offering prayer'. © Brian Wren.
'Easter affirmation and prayer'. © Brian Wren.
'Easter praise'. © Brian Wren.

Litanies

'Fasting'. © S. Wesley Ariarajah.
'Break forth together into singing!' © S. Wesley Ariarajah.
'The movement of the Spirit'. © S. Wesley Ariarajah & Lindsey Sanderson.

Symbolic Acts

'Loving God'. © Lindsey Sanderson.
'Come Holy Spirit'. © Lindsey Sanderson.
'Forgiveness and reconciliation'. © Cathy Bott.

Complete Liturgies

'A service of word and table'. © Brian Wren.

PART 3: LOVING SERVICE

Hymns and Songs

'The washing of the feet'. Words & music: © Jaci C. Maraschin. Translation:
  by Brian Wren, © CWM.
'Jesus Christ sets free to serve'. Words: theme song, CCA 8th General
  Assembly, 1985; music: © I-to Loh.
'If we love one another'. Words: based on 1 John 4:12. Music: © 1998 I-to Loh.
'Christ's freedom meal'. Words: extracted from Brian Wren's hymn, 'There's a
  Spirit in the Air', © 1969, 1995 Stainer & Bell Ltd for the World except
  USA, Canada, Australia and New Zealand. Reprinted by permission. Music:
  © 1998 I-to Loh.
'Guaicuru kyrie'. Words: Simei Monteiro. Music: the Guaicuru people, Brazil,
  adapted by Simei Monteiro, 1993. Portuguese translation and arrangement ©
  2000 General Board of Global Ministries, GBGMusik, 475 Riverside Drive,
  New York, NY 10115, USA. All rights reserved. Used by permission.
'Loku Famba/Look around you'. Words & music: © Arao Litsure.
'A Christmas hymn'. Words: Andrew Williams; music: Traditional.

Calls to Worship

'We are the hands of Christ'. © Brian Wren.

Prayers

'A litany of intercession'. © Brian Wren.
'Christ, you meet us'. Words: © Brian Wren. Music: © 1998 I-to Loh.
'I will follow you wherever you go.' © Francis Brienen.
'The word made flesh'. © Francis Brienen.
'Prayer of Intercession'. © Andrew Williams.
'Closing Prayer'. © Lindsey Sanderson.

Symbolic Acts

'The circle of love'. © Brian Wren.
'What is love?' © Lindsey Sanderson.

Stories and Dramas

'The giving tree'. © Shel Silverstein. Taken from *The Second European
  Ecumenical Assembly Worship Book*, CEC & CCEE, 1997.
'Who is my neighbour?' © Lindsey Sanderson.
'Stories from Penrhys'. © Lindsey Sanderson.
'Bearing one another's burdens'. © Cathy Bott.

Complete Liturgies

'In Jesus' footsteps'. © Simei Monteiro.

PART 4: NURTURING AND TEACHING

Hymns and Songs

'We meet as friends at table'. Words: Brian Wren, © 1996 Stainer & Bell Ltd
for the World except USA, Canada, Australia and New Zealand. Reprinted
by permission. Music: Hal Hopson, © 1996 Hope Publishing Co.,
administered by CopyCare, PO Box 77, Hailsham, BN27 3EF, UK.

'Many yet one are the gifts of God's people'. Words: © 1998 Lindsey
Sanderson. Music: Susan Heafield, © 1999 Praise Partners Publishing.

'Remember'. Words & music: © Noel Dexter.

'The church is like a table'. Words: Fred Kaan, © 1985 Hope Publishing Co. for
USA and Canada, and Stainer & Bell Ltd for all other territories. Music: ©
1997 I-to Loh.

'Tua palavra é lâmpada'. Words & music: Simei Monteiro. Words & music ©
2000 General Board of Global Ministries, GBGMusik, 475 Riverside Drive,
New York, NY 10115, USA. All rights reserved. Used by permission.

'You are my body'. Words: Brian Wren, © 1993 Stainer & Bell Ltd for the
World except USA, Canada, Australia and New Zealand. Reprinted by
permission. Music: John Horman, © 1998 Hope Publishing Co.,
administered by CopyCare, PO Box 77, Hailsham, BN27 3EF, UK.

'Here's a new robe'. Words: © Brian Wren. Music: Susan Heafield, © 1999
Praise Partners Publishing.

'Holy God, as you love us'. Words: Brian Wren. Music: Susan Heafield. Words
& music © 1999 Praise Partners Publishing. All rights reserved.

'Swamin wahanse'. Words: transcription from the Sinhalese original © I-to Loh.
Music: from the Sri Lankan Liturgy.

Calls to Worship

'Fed by community . . .' © Lindsey Sanderson.

'Living in the unity . . .' © Lindsey Sanderson.

'People of the Covenant, draw near'. © Brian Wren.

Prayers

'An invitation to the banquet'. © Francis Brienen.

'Living One, we belong to you'. © Brian Wren.

'May the Lover of Creation . . .' © Brian Wren.

'Christ, our Teacher'. © Brian Wren.

'An opening prayer'. © Brian Wren.

'A prayer of confession'. © CWM (Chorus by Susan Heafield.)

'The road to Emmaus'. © Francis Brienen.

Stories and Dramas

'The story of the hand'. © Lindsey Sanderson.

'The rainbow'. © *The Second European Ecumenical Assembly Worship Book*,
ibid. Adapted by Lindsey Sanderson.

Complete Liturgies

'We all belong to Christ's body'. © I-to Loh. *Includes:*
'If one member suffers'. Music © 1998 I-to Loh.
'If we love one another'. Music © 1998 I-to Loh.
'Swamin wahanse'. Transcription from the Sinhalese original © I-to Loh. Music
   from the Sri Lankan Liturgy.
'The Lord has told us what is good'. Music © 1995 I-to Loh.
'Karen benediction'. Translated by Anna May. Traditional Burmese melody,
'Mar ba zey'. Reprinted by permission of I-to Loh.
'A communion meditation'. © Simei Monteiro & Lindsey Sanderson.

PART 5: CARING FOR THE CREATION

Hymns and Songs

'The God of us all'. Words: © Ron O'Grady. Music: © I-to Loh.
'Thank you, God, for water, soil and air'. Words: Brian Wren, © 1975 Stainer
   & Bell Limited for the World except USA, Canada, Australia and New
   Zealand. © Hope Publishing Company in the USA. Music: John Weaver,
   Copyright © 1990 Hope Publishing Company, administered by CopyCare,
   PO Box 77, Hailsham, BN27 3EF, UK, used by permission.
'Send out your Spirit'. Words: Brian Wren, © Council for World Mission.
   Music: © Simei Monteiro.
'God's glory (praise)'. Words: Brian Wren. Music: Susan Heafield. Words &
   music © 1999 Praise Partners Publishing. All rights reserved.
'Earth is abused (repentance)'. Words: Brian Wren. Music: Susan Heafield.
   Words & music © 1999 Praise Partners Publishing. All rights reserved.
'Can we believe . . .? (thanksgiving)'. Words: Brian Wren. Music: Susan
   Heafield. Words & music © 1999 Praise Partners Publishing. All rights
   reserved.
'We praise you, O God'. Words & music: © Noel Dexter.
'O forgive us, dear Lord'. Words & music: © Noel Dexter.
'We praise you, we thank you'. Words & music: © Noel Dexter.
'Loving God forgive'. Words & music: © Andrew Williams.

Calls to Worship

'The earth belongs to God'. © Brian Wren.
'Our Creator calls us'. © Brian Wren.
'In the beginning God said . . .' © Cathy Bott.

Prayers

'A prayer of confession'. © Cathy Bott.
'A prayer of commitment'. © Cathy Bott.
'Bright and beautiful God'. © Francis Brienen.

Litanies

'A litany on creation'. © S. Wesley Ariarajah.

Symbolic Acts

'Modelling'. © Lindsey Sanderson.

Stories and Dramas

'Miss World visits the doctor'. © Lindsey Sanderson.
'Greyfriars Bobby'. © Lindsey Sanderson.